VARIATIONS
COOKBOOK
QUICK RECIPES

Abbreviations and Quantities

1 oz	= 1 ounce = 28 grams
1 lb	= 1 pound = 16 ounces
1 cup	= approx. 5-8 ounces * (depending on density)
1 cup	= 8 fluid ounces = 250 milliliters (liquids)
2 cups	= 1 pint (liquids)
8 pints	= 4 quarts = 1 gallon (liquids)
1 g	= 1 gram = $1/1000$ kilogram
1 kg	= 1 kilogram = 1000 grams = $2^{1}/_{4}$ lb
1 l	= 1 liter = 1000 milliliters (ml) = approx. 34 fluid ounces
125 milliliters (ml)	= approx. 8 tablespoons = $^{1}/_{2}$ cup
1 tbsp	= 1 level tablespoon = 15-20 g * (depending on density);
	= 15 milliliters (liquids)
1 tsp	= 1 level teaspoon = 3-5 g * (depending on density) = 5 ml (liquids)

*The weight of dry ingredients varies significantly depending on the density factor, e.g. 1 cup flour weighs less than 1 cup butter. Quantities in ingredients have been rounded up or down for convenience, where appropriate. Metric conversions may therefore not correspond exactly. It is important to use either American or metric measurements within a recipe.

British Cookery Terms

US	UK	US	UK
arugula	rocket (rocket salad)	molasses	treacle
bacon slices	streaky bacon, streaky rashers	offal	variety meats
beet	beetroot	papaya	pawpaw
bouillon cube	stock cube	parsley root	Hamburg parsley
broil, broiler	grill, oven grill	peanut, peanut oil	groundnut, groundnut oil
chicory	endive	pit	stone (of fruits)
cilantro	fresh coriander leaves	porcini mushrooms	ceps, boletus or penny bun
coconut, shredded or grated	desiccated coconut	powdered sugar	icing sugar
cookie	biscuit (sweet)	rise	prove
corn	maize, sweetcorn	rutabaga	Swede
cornstarch	cornflour	seed	pip
eggplant	aubergine	shrimp	prawn
flour, all-purpose	plain flour	slivered almonds	flaked almonds
French fries	chips	snow peas, sugar peas	mangetout
golden raisins	sultanas	Swiss chard	chard
grill	barbecue	tart	flan
ground beef or pork	minced meat or mince	tofu	beancurd
ham (cured)	gammon	tomato paste	tomato puree
heavy (whipping) cream	double cream	whole wheat	wholemeal
jelly	jam	zucchini	courgette

© h.f.ullmann publishing GmbH
Original title: *Variationenkochbuch. Blitzschnelle Rezepte*
ISBN of the original edition: 978-3-8331-6381-4
Design, photography, layout, and typesetting: TLC Digitales Fotostudio GmbH & Co KG, Velen-Ramsdorf
Text and recipes: Sylvia Winnewisser
Copy editing: Annerose Sieck
Editorial assistance: Claudia Boss-Teichmann

© for this English edition:
h.f.ullmann publishing GmbH

Translation from German: Sarah Smith in association with First Edition Translations Ltd, Cambridge, UK
Editing: Sally Heavens in association with First Edition Translations Ltd, Cambridge, UK
Typesetting: Rob Partington in association with First Edition Translations Ltd, Cambridge, UK
Cover design: Hubert Hepfinger
Overall responsibility for production: h.f.ullmann publishing GmbH, Potsdam, Germany

ISBN 978-3-8480-0009-8

Printed in China

10 9 8 7 6 5 4 3 2 1
X IX VIII VII VI V IV III II I

www.ullmann-publishing.com
newsletter@ullmann-publishing.com

VARIATIONS
COOKBOOK

QUICK RECIPES

More than 200 basic recipes and variations

h.f.ullmann

CONTENTS

Introduction 6

Appetizers 18

Pasta, potatoes, etc. 60

Meat, poultry, and fish 90

Desserts 132

Index of recipes 158

INTRODUCTION

This book is a source of inspiration and help for anyone who, despite being short on time, still wants to enjoy imaginative and varied food.

We understand you may prefer to jump in and get started, but please take time to read through this Introduction. You'll find tips on storing food, as well as other useful information that will help you save valuable time later on.

So, have fun cooking, and bon appétit!

ABOUT THIS BOOK

Quick and healthy

As the saying goes, time is money! We live in a hectic world where everything has to be done in a rush. Sometimes, this includes cooking and preparing our food.

We don't always have the time or the desire to go shopping after a full day's work, let alone create a full menu. At the same time, we must not keep resorting to fast food. Not only do burgers, fries, etc. make us put on weight, they contain very few vitamins and minerals. In the long run, they actually starve our bodies of essential nutrients.

We are all much better off preparing quick and simple dishes containing fresh vegetables, meat, or fish, with plenty of time afterward to make a quick dessert and spend time with our family and friends.

Maybe you're in the process of planning a small party with a buffet, a barbecue, or a picnic. You don't fancy spending hours in the kitchen beforehand, but still want to offer your guests something a little bit special... No problem. You'll find everything you're looking for, here in this book. Not only does it contain

numerous recipes for simple snacks, appetizers, desserts, soups, and salads, it also gives you delicious ideas for unique creations with meat, potatoes, pasta, and rice.

Step by step

Here's how it works. This book is divided into four chapters: appetizers; dishes made with pasta, potatoes etc.; recipes using meat, poultry, and fish; and, finally, desserts and drinks. There's something for all occasions and tastes. Whether it is a quick family lunch or dinner, a romantic meal for two, a big get-together with friends, or a more intimate birthday celebration—we have so many ideas, you will never struggle to create a quick, healthy meal ever again!

Each recipe features a basic (and mostly traditional) method—something you may have always wanted to learn about in detail. You'll also find clear, step by step instructions and photographs, as well as more in-depth information about specific ingredients, cooking techniques, and recipes for complementary side dishes.

Recipe variations

This book starts exactly where other cookery books stop—with recipe variations.

This means that, not only will you find a recipe for preparing a wok dish, for example, but on the following double-page spread you'll also find four to six variations on the dish, each with a clear and detailed photograph. As a bonus, we also show you extras, such as different types of bread, potatoes, rice, pasta, polenta, vegetables, and salad. We also recommend dips and sauces for you to experiment with, and even change to your own taste. We want to introduce you to the best variations on each basic recipe so that you have as wide a range of dishes as possible

to choose from. To do this, we've tried a few different avenues for some themes. For certain recipes, we introduce you to a basic technique you can adopt and repeat for the variations. For others, we give you one main recipe and about four to six independent variations. Also, in our experience, some recipe variations can only be combined with certain side dishes, sauces, and dips, which we will clearly point out to you. Although you are, of course, free to create whole new taste sensations yourself!

We also show you a wide selection of

tasty morsels to try out alongside dishes as and when you feel like them, plus handy tips and information on individual ingredients. All the dishes shown in this book can be made in 30 minutes or less, including preparation time. Some jobs, e.g. cooking potatoes to be used in a salad, can of course be carried out the evening before, to save even more time.

However you choose to use this book, good luck—and have fun experimenting!

Side dishes

We've tried to keep a balance when choosing side dishes. While the first section mainly sticks to salads, dips, and spreads as accompaniments, the second contains more filling ones for meat, poultry, and fish. We include a few grain-based side dishes, such as polenta and couscous, as well as others featuring potatoes, rice, sauces, dips, and chutneys. In the desserts chapter, you'll discover treats

such as cakes, flans, mousses, creams, fruit sauces, and drinks. As a rule, we've avoided providing the exact quantities of ingredients for side dishes, as they are merely intended as suggestions. But here are a few tips... Stick to about 28 oz (800 g) for potatoes, 14 oz (400 g) for pasta, and about 9 oz (250 g) for rice, cornmeal, bulgur, and couscous (all when cooking for 4 people). For the rest, you will need to experiment, to see whether you prefer to add 1 or 2 onions, 2 or 3 bell peppers, 4 or 5 oz (100 or 150 g) mushrooms to the rice, couscous, or pasta, or 5 or 7 tablespoons of grated Parmesan to the polenta.

Time-saving foods

It is virtually impossible to be creative when you're tired and hungry. You just want to eat, there and then, without all the preparation. Besides storing food correctly (see pages 12–13), convenience foods are a recipe for success when it comes to preparing food quickly. Nowadays, these are available as both conventional and organic foods, and it pays to have some at the ready to save even more time.

Canned and frozen foods are ready to eat, and only need to be heated up and served with side dishes or other ingredients.

To make cooking as quick and simple as possible, use canned beans, lentils, and chickpeas. They only need to be rinsed with cold water and drained in a colander, before being used in various ways. We also recommend using canned tomatoes, particularly those dishes that have tomato-based sauces. Because they are harvested and preserved when fully ripe, canned tomatoes often have a more intense flavor than their fresh, unripe counterparts. Many types of vegetables, e.g. spinach, beans, and peas, can be bought frozen and still be of good quality. Their nutrients are mostly well preserved and you

don't need to spend time cleaning them.

The same goes for herbs and some fruits. For example, raspberries are ideal bought frozen, as they develop their full flavor when thawed and can be made into delicious desserts.

Skinning and filleting fish all takes time, particularly when you're not experienced at it. You can find all the most popular varieties prepared and ready to eat in the frozen food section of the supermarket. For example, fillets need only to be cut into bite-size pieces. It is a similar situation with meat. In some cases, e.g., dishes using strips of meat, all the work is done for you. You can

buy meat strips, skewers, and other prepared meat products both fresh from supermarket meat counters and pre-packed.

INFO QUANTITIES

In this book you will find that the ingredients are always given in Imperial (American) measurements followed by the Metric equivalent. See page 2 for a conversion table and explanation of the abbreviations.

Quality of products

One thing to bear in mind when thinking about the quality of food is that salad, vegetables, fruit, and

cereals that have been grown outdoors and without the use of chemical additives (e.g. organic) are naturally healthier and easier to digest than those that are grown in greenhouses and fertilized, treated, or fumigated with chemical agents (not to mention GM products, which should be avoided completely.) The same applies for rice, pasta, dairy products, fish, meat, and poultry. As a result, when buying fresh produce we recommend choosing fruit and vegetables that are in season, and available on the domestic market wherever possible. We have to remember that the residues of chemical

substances are stored in salad and vegetables, and transfer to us when we eat them.

High quality and tasty meat does not come from huge factory farms, neither is it sold at bargain prices. If it's good steak you want, buy branded or organic meat products.

Some more advice for fish and seafood... When buying both fresh and frozen fish, check whether it has come from sustainable fisheries and aquaculture. The Marine Stewardship Council (MSC) is an independent

charitable organization, whose purpose is to protect fish and seafood stock from over-fishing. The MSC Seal is only awarded to products that protect endangered fish stocks and their ecosystem. Please look at the packaging of frozen fish to see if it bears the MSC label, and ask for it when buying from the fresh fish counter. In respect of organic aquaculture, fewer fish are bred within one area than in conventional fisheries, and their diet is carefully controlled. Finally, when buying tuna, make sure it is dolphin friendly!

Hints and tips for shopping

When buying salad, vegetables, and fruit, make sure they are fresh. How can you tell? Fruit and vegetables should be firm. They shouldn't soften or sound hollow when handled. Salad leaves should be firm and juicy, and not hang down limply. The cut points are important and should still be damp, which means that the vegetable/salad was harvested that day. Freshness is particularly important in the case of asparagus. Moreover, vegetables/salad should have no

brown spots or stains, and green vegetables such as broccoli should not be yellow. Some types of vegetables are better when bought smaller, e.g. zucchini. The larger vegetables often have fibrous, bland-tasting flesh. For some types of fruit, such as melon and pineapple, it pays to have

a quick sniff. Those with an aromatic smell are ripe.

STORAGE

Weekly menu

Why not sit down with your family and make a game out of putting together a weekly menu? Everyone can take their favorite recipe from the book and make a contribution. Once you have a weekly menu and everyone is happy, writing a shopping list couldn't be simpler.

Not only is shopping less hectic when you have a list to hand, it also works out cheaper, because the only items that end up in your shopping cart are those that you need, with no extras. The work can be shared out, too. One person can fetch fresh ingredients from the market while the others take care of the wrapped or longer-lasting products.

If you are organized, plan shopping trips properly, and invest in a good stock of long-life ingredients and frozen produce, you'll be able to prepare delicious meals with minimum effort and save more adventurous dishes for the weekend.

A number of basic ingredients such as vegetables, pasta, rice, etc. can be pre-cooked and then used throughout the week in a variety of different recipes. For example, home-made tomato sauce can be served with spaghetti, and also used as a sauce for quick vegetable lasagna. A mix of vegetables can be used as a side dish for meat, or as a filler for soups. A number of vegetables such as broccoli, cauliflower, and carrots taste just as good freshly cooked as in creamy soups.

Storage

It's advisable to keep a number of different foods in stock at home all the time, so that you can quickly and easily follow our recipes or recipe variations whenever you like. Here are our suggestions:

Dried goods:

– salt (sea salt); black and white peppercorns (whole or ground); nutmeg; caraway; ground paprika; curry powder; cayenne; cinnamon sticks; cloves
– dried herbes de Provence; thyme; oregano; marjoram; rosemary; bay leaves; pizza herbs; salad herbs
– all-purpose flour; cornstarch
– pasta; different durum wheat and/or wholemeal varieties; egg noodles
– rice, e.g. long-grain, pudding, risotto, wholegrain, basmati, jasmine; quick-cook rice
– rice noodles

– couscous; bulgur; cornmeal (for polenta)
– sugar, granulated; confectioners' sugar; vanilla sugar
– dried fruit, as required
– bouillon cubes / gravy powder
– ready to cook sauces, in different flavors
– dried breadcrumbs
– dried mushrooms, e.g. bolete
– fried pulses, e.g. peas; lentils (green, yellow, red, black); white and red beans; chickpeas.

Vinegar, oil, mayonnaise, etc.:

- honey
- mustard, e.g. hot, mild, with or without grains
- vinegar, e.g. balsamic vinegar, dark and light, red/white wine vinegar, fruit vinegar, sherry vinegar, raspberry vinegar

- oil, e.g. cooking oil for frying, olive/sunflower/rapeseed/grape/pumpkin seed oil for salads and adding flavor, all cold pressed
- butter; margarine
- seasoning sauces such as ketchup, rémoulade, soy sauce (light and dark), Tabasco® Sauce, Worcestershire sauce, oyster sauce, tomato purée
- mayonnaise
- stock, e.g. chicken/fish/meat/vegetable stock
- cream; crème fraîche; heavy sour cream/sour cream
- alcohol for cooking, e.g. red wine; white wine; brandy; port; sherry; Noilly Prat; grappa; Marsala; Amaretto.

Canned food:

- canned tomatoes (chopped and whole); puréed tomatoes; tomato juice; gherkins
- capers
- olives (green, black)
- tuna
- beans (white, red)
- sweet corn
- chickpeas
- artichoke hearts

Fresh ingredients:

It's always a good idea to have the following fresh ingredients to hand, too:
- potatoes
- onions (shallots, red and white onions)
- lemons (or bottled lemon juice)
- eggs
- chiles
- bread (baguette, white or toasting, crispbread, wholemeal)
- vegetables as desired, e.g. tomatoes, carrots
- salad (available ready-washed and chopped for those in a real hurry)
- ready-made salad dressing for emergencies
- Parmesan (block, or ready grated)
- mozzarella (packed)
- ewe's milk cheese (packed).

Frozen foods:

We also recommend keeping a stock of certain foods in the freezer:

Frozen products such as fish fillets, seafood, chicken, vegetables, fruit (all depending on taste), bread and/or bread rolls for baking, puff pastry, and ready-made pizza dough. If you stock your larder or cupboards following these suggestions, you'll already have a lot of the ingredients needed to follow our recipes, and will then just need to buy the final main ingredient(s) fresh.

Preserving food

Just 30 years ago, a lot of households used to have sterilizing equipment for preserving food. This has all been forgotten, now that we have freezers. Nevertheless, certain old preservation methods such as soaking food in oil, vinegar, or alcohol have regained

popularity, simply because homemade food tastes delicious. The main purpose of making preserves used to be to make food from summer and fall last through the winter months. Nowadays, we do it to experiment with different flavors. To start with, fans of quick and easy meals are a little shocked at how long it takes. Yet much of it can be done more quickly than it might appear, and

the time you invest will later pay off when you can simply go to a cup-board and add a few goodies to your meals such as antipasti or mixed pickles.

Cooking techniques

Gently cooking a roast in the oven at 175 °F/80 °C isn't suitable for quick meals, as the cooking process takes several hours. Let's take a brief look at cooking techniques:

Blanching
Blanching involves placing vegetables in boiling water for a few minutes,

then taking them out and plunging them into ice water to halt the cooking process. This technique retains the green color of vegetables (e.g. beans and broccoli). Blanched vegetables can then be used for salads, or stuffed (e.g. cabbage leaves). All vegetables are suitable for blanching, with the exception of mushrooms.

Stewing
Stewing involves briefly browning small pieces of vegetable, fish, meat,

or poultry in a little hot fat, and then simmering gently in a liquid such as stock, water, or wine. Besides steaming, this is one of the healthiest cooking techniques.

Poaching

Poaching is particularly suited to fish fillets and fish steaks, as these require little cooking time. They can be poached in a small amount of hot liquid. Individual pieces can also be poached directly in a sauce—for example, in a curry or mustard sauce.

Steaming

Steaming is actually the most gentle and healthy way of cooking vegetables and fish. Food placed in a steamer cooks using steam and uses no fat whatsoever. This particular method is best for preserving the color, texture, and flavor of food, as well as all of its nutrients. All vegetables and fish with firm flesh are suitable for steaming.

Boiling

Boiling involves placing vegetables, fish, meat, and poultry in boiling stock or salt water and, depending on the variety, cooking them until they are either tender or still firm (al dente), as required. Various vegetables are peeled beforehand, although beet is better left untouched as it can bleed. Potatoes can be boiled with or without their skins. You can boil any type of vegetables, fish, seafood, muscle meat, and poultry. Green beans must be cooked this way, as they are poisonous if eaten raw. Potatoes and vegetables should be just covered with water. Pasta, rice, and cereals are boiled in salt water or stock. Pasta should be al dente after cooking.

Braising

Vegetables, meat, and poultry are sweated for a few minutes in a pan with a small quantity of fat. Then some kind of liquid is added, such as bouillon, water, cooking juices, wine, or cream, and the food is cooked over low heat. When braising, you can also use butter, oil, and clarified butter, and all types of vegetable are suitable.

Sautéing

Sautéing involves cooking meat in a pan for a relatively short period of time, depending on the desired degree of cooking. It is especially suited to cooking slices of meat such as steaks, schnitzels, and chops. Strips of meat and meatballs can also be cooked in a pan, although it's important to ensure that they are well cooked all the way through, just as when cooking poultry. Meat will cook faster if kept at room temperature beforehand. If this is not the case, too much liquid will escape and the meat will dry out. Pieces of meat should be seasoned after frying.

Stir-frying

This technique of cooking in a pan

originates from Asia, where vegetables are eaten while still very crunchy and crisp. The preferred piece of equipment in this instance is the wok. Vegetable pieces are cooked in hot oil for 2–3 minutes (stirring continuously) and then pushed to the edges to drain. All types of vegetables are suitable for stir-frying. Fish, meat, and poultry can also be cut into strips or cubes and sautéed in a wok.

Baking

Meat, poultry, and fish can be cooked in the oven, although only fish and stuffed vegetables cook quickly.

Gratinating

Gratinating involves adding a crunchy crust to meat, poultry, fish, or vegetable dishes that have already been cooked: for example, a topping of cheese, or a mixture of butter and various spices or nuts. This can be done either in the oven or under the broiler. The desired amount of topping should be spread over the food and heated until the cheese has melted and/or the crust is golden brown.

Grilling

Grilling involves cooking pieces of vegetable, meat, fish, and poultry on a rack over the heat source: hardwood, charcoal, gas, or electric. Alternatively, it can be done in a stove-top grill. No fat is required and you will still get the distinctive "grill stripes." The taste, however, is not quite the same as that of food grilled in the "proper" way. Grilling is suited to zucchini, bell peppers, eggplant, tomatoes, artichokes, black salsify, and mushrooms, as well as sausages, chops, steaks, whole fish, seafood, chicken legs, and chicken wings. Food can be brushed with a marinade or oil before grilling, to prevent it from drying out.

Frying

A lot of vegetables, fish, meat, and

poultry—and even fruit—can be fried, if coated in a batter or beer batter beforehand. Fruit and vegetables stay crisp and juicy, and the outer crust becomes crunchy. Pieces of fish, meat, and poultry also stay tender, when cooked in this way.

The right tools

It goes without saying that even the quickest recipes will take longer to follow without reasonable cooking facilities and tools. A good cooker and decent pots and pans are essential, too. And if the whole process is still too slow for you, having the right appliances can ensure maximum time saving. A pressure cooker cuts cooking times by up to 70 percent and is especially good when cooking larger quantities. An electric citrus press gives you an extra speed boost when squeezing oranges, limes, and lemons. But what good is all that if your knives are blunt? A speedy recipe will turn into a tedious ordeal. Sharp knives are absolutely essential. Buy larger ones for chopping meat and vegetables, and smaller ones for peeling and dicing fruit, for example. You'll also need a vegetable peeler (and one for asparagus), a serrated knife for chopping onions, garlic, and herbs, a mandoline for thinly slicing cucumber and making julienne carrots, etc., and a grater for vegetables and cheese.

Good knives are worth the investment, there's no doubt about it. And, once you've bought them, they should last a lifetime. Their high quality will ensure you work quickly and smoothly with all the foodstuffs found in a kitchen.

Cook once, eat for days

If, after trying a few things out, you discover a favorite recipe, you can double or even triple the ingredients and freeze a few portions. There are bound to be days when even 30 minutes is too long to prepare food. This is when you can go to the freezer first thing in the morning and take out your or your family's favorite food, ready to simply warm it up in the evening and maybe serve a quick side dish with it (or even just bread).

If you cook regularly for people who

love tomato sauce, it's sensible to make several portions and freeze it. Pesto fans can prepare larger quantities, too, as it will keep fresh for a good week or so in sealed jars. The same goes for many types of vinaigrette, which you can use with salads several times a week. You'll find lots of ideas for sauces, dips, dressings, vinaigrettes, etc. in this

book. Once you've discovered your favorites, you can quickly make some more. Don't forget to label cans, jars, and other containers.

It's important to write the date on jars. In the case of frozen food portions, make a note of exactly what is inside.

If, one day, you've forgotten to take something out of the freezer and have no choice but to serve up a ready-meal, there are still things you can do to pep it up a little. Fresh herbs, which you should always keep in stock whenever possible (they keep up to a week in freezer bags in the vegetable drawer of the icebox) will add flavor to any meal. If all you have to hand is a pack of frozen vegetables, spice them up with cabanossi, bologna, frankfurters, or salami. That works with mozzarella and ewe's milk cheese, of course; even a boiled or fried egg can be made in a matter of minutes. Nuts and seeds can also be added to bland ready-meals for extra flavor.

And what about when guests appear on your doorstep out of the blue? Cook something easy and something you're familiar with. After all, now is not the time to be experimenting. Take a look in your cupboards—you're bound to have a pack of spaghetti, tomato sauce, and dried herbs. And, if you have eggs, bacon, and cream, you

can easily whip up scrambled egg or a carbonara sauce. If your guests are potato lovers, slice some of the vegetables thinly and bake with a cream and cheese mixture for delicious potatoes au gratin.

APPETIZERS

Delicious appetizers, tasty soups, and elegant snacks— these dishes are popular, quick to prepare, and perfect for special occasions.

Skewers, pancake rolls, and crostini, etc. are bound to make a good impression, whether for a picnic, party, or buffet.

Served with the right dips and side dishes, they'll be a hit with family and friends. What's more, all the following dishes can be prepared in 30 minutes or less.

GRILLED SKEWERS
with marinated chicken breast

GINGER INFO

Ginger has a spicy, pungent flavor that gives dishes a distinctive aroma. Although it has always played a major role in Asian cuisine, it has now gained popularity here as well. Fresh ginger should always be firm and smooth. The best way to use it is to take a small piece of root, scrape off the skin, and grate the flesh. It can also be cut into thin slices, diced, or pushed through a garlic press. Ginger powder has a completely different smell and so is no substitute for fresh ginger.

Serves 4

14 oz (400 g)	chicken breast fillets
2 tbsp	sesame oil
2 tbsp	soy sauce
1 tbsp	Noilly Prat vermouth
1 tsp	grated ginger
1/2 tsp	curry powder
1/2 tsp	sugar
	Salt
	Pepper
20 min.	marinating time
30 min.	preparation time

Step by step

Wash the chicken breast fillets then remove the skin and tendons.

Mix together the sesame oil, soy sauce, vermouth, ginger, curry powder, sugar, salt and pepper to make a marinade.

Place the chicken breast in the marinade and leave to stand for approximately 20 minutes.

Remove the meat from the marinade, drain, and cut into cubes.

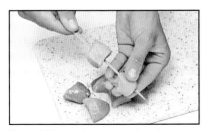

Place chicken cubes on wooden skewers and bake in the oven at 425 °F/220 °C for 15 minutes.

Dip

To make **peanut dip**, sweat 1 diced onion until soft in 1 tablespoon of butter. Add $^2/_3$ cup (150 g) peanut butter and generous $^3/_4$ cup (200 ml) milk, bring to the boil, and stir in 1 tablespoon of soy sauce. Leave to cool and serve with chicken skewers.

Salad

To make **green salad with tomatoes**, wash 1 head of oak leaf lettuce, dry in a salad spinner, and tear into small pieces. Place in bowl with 2 diced tomatoes and 2 chopped red onions. Prepare a dressing using 2 tablespoons white wine vinegar, 3 tablespoons olive oil, 1 teaspoon mustard, salt and pepper, and mix with the salad. Sprinkle with chopped parsley.

GRILLED SKEWERS
several variations

Not only can these tasty grilled skewers be prepared in a number of different ways, they're also ideal for a number of different occasions. Serve freshly grilled at barbecues, cold at picnics or buffets, or with salad at home as a delicious appetizer. Here are some variations.

Preparation time: 30 minutes

... with chicken, chile, and mushrooms

Dice 14 oz (400 g) chicken then season with salt and pepper. Wash and pat dry 4 small red chiles. Clean 24 small mushrooms with a damp cloth. Alternate the chicken cubes, chiles, and mushrooms on wooden skewers. Brush with rosemary oil and cook in the oven at 425 °F/220 °C for 15 minutes.

Preparation time: 25 minutes

... with shrimp, garlic, and lemongrass

Soak 12 shrimp in a marinade of 2 teaspoons honey, 3 tablespoons white wine, 1 teaspoon vinegar, 2 tablespoons gin, salt, and pepper for 15 minutes. Pat dry. Cut 4 lemongrass stalks to a point at the bottom to make skewers. Alternate 3 shrimp and 2 half cloves garlic on each skewer. Grill over electric heat for 7 minutes.

Preparation time: 25 minutes

... with fish, cherry tomatoes, and zucchini

Dice 1¼ lb (600 g) redfish fillets and wrap in halved slices of bacon. Alternate on wooden skewers with 1 zucchini cut into 1-in. (2.4-cm) slices and 12 cherry tomatoes. Mix together 4 tablespoons olive oil and 1 tablespoon sherry vinegar, 2 tablespoons Worcestershire sauce, 1 tablespoon chopped cilantro, salt, and pepper. Brush the skewers and grill over electric heat for 10 minutes.

Preparation time: 30 minutes

... with turkey breast, artichokes, and olives

Dice 14 oz (400 g) turkey breast fillets and soak in a marinade of 3 tablespoons olive oil, 2 tablespoons sherry, 1 tablespoon herbes de Provence, salt, and pepper. Drain and alternate on wooden skewers with 4 halved artichoke hearts from a jar and 16 pitted black olives. Cook in the oven at 425 °F/220 °C for 15 minutes.

DIPS
for skewers

Serve the skewers shown here with the right dip and they'll taste even better.

Preparation time: 30 minutes

... with pork and scallions

Brush 14 oz (400 g) cubed pork loin with a marinade of 3 table-spoons white wine, 2 tablespoons peanut oil, 1 tablespoon mustard, salt, paprika, and pepper. Dice the light green parts of 8 scallions with 1 red bell pepper. Alternate the meat, scallions, and bell peppers on skewers and grill over electric heat for 20 minutes.

Preparation time: 30 minutes

... with mixed vegetables

Wash and halve 1 small eggplant, 1 zucchini, and 1 yellow bell pepper and cut into 1-in. (2.4-cm) pieces. Peel and quarter 4 red onions. Alternate vegetables on skewers with cherry tomatoes. Season with salt and pepper and drizzle with olive oil. Grill over electric heat for 20 minutes.

Garlic dip

Mix together chopped onion, pressed garlic, yogurt, mayonnaise, olive oil, lemon juice, salt, and pepper. Perfect with vegetable and meat skewers.

Herb dip

Combine mixed, chopped herbs, with yogurt, olive oil, lemon juice, salt, and pepper. Perfect with recipe variations.

Yogurt and lemon dip

Mix together Greek yogurt, chopped preserved lemons, chopped garlic, olive oil, chopped chiles, paprika, chopped dill, and salt. Perfect with fish and shrimp.

CARPACCIO
with beef and Parmesan

	Serves 4
9 oz (250 g)	*beef fillet*
	Salt
1	*lemon*
3 tbsp	*olive oil*
	Freshly ground pepper
1³/₄ oz (50) g	*Parmesan*
	Cress to garnish
20 min.	*preparation time*

Step by step

Wash the beef fillet, pat dry, and freeze.

Halve the lemon and drizzle the juice over the sliced meat.

Take the meat out of the freezer. Cut into wafer-thin slices with a very sharp knife.

Sprinkle with olive oil, season with freshly ground black pepper, and top with Parmesan shavings.

Arrange the slices of beef on a lightly salted platter.

Garnish with cress leaves and serve.

PARMESAN INFO

Grana Parmigiano-Reggiano, to give it its full name, is a hard granular cheese, with a fat in dry matter content of 35 percent. Originating from Emilia Romagna

and Parma, Parmesan is made from raw cow's milk, traditionally between April and October. Large cheese wheels are left to mature for at least six months before being sold. Parmesan is often used for sprinkling over carpaccio and pasta, but also used to make pesto and to add a tasty crust to gratin dishes. Nevertheless, it tastes even better eaten on its own with fresh bread, olives and wine, or as a dessert with fresh fruit.

CRESS INFO

Cress belongs to the cabbage family and comes in several different forms. Garden cress is known as a small-leaved herb; it is used as a garnish for salads, vegetable, poultry, and fish dishes as well as an ingredient

for herbal preparations, and has a slightly tangy flavour. Watercress has a more peppery taste and larger leaves, while the bright red flowers of nasturtium are not only good to look at, but are also edible.

SAUCES
to serve with carpaccio

Sauces are the icing on the cake for any type of carpaccio. Here are three, made with milk, tuna, and tangy vinaigrette. Don't forget bread for dipping!

Lemon mayonnaise
Mix together mayonnaise, Worcestershire sauce, lemon juice, milk, salt, and pepper. Perfect with veal and beef carpaccio.

Tuna sauce
Blend together tuna, mayonnaise, meat bouillon, anchovies, capers, salt, and pepper. Perfect with veal and turkey breast carpaccio.

Vinaigrette
Mix together chopped scallions, pressed garlic, wine vinegar, walnut oil, salt, and pepper. Perfect with all recipe variations.

CARPACCIO
several

An appetizer for food connoisseurs! Originally from Italy, this appetizer has become a firm favorite all over the world. It therefore comes as no surprise that it's made in all sorts of different ways now, besides using beef. And since the ingredients are mainly raw

Preparation time: 30 minutes

... with veal and capers
Freeze 14 oz (400 g) veal, cut into thin slices, and arrange on a platter. Finely dice 1 red and 1 green bell pepper and 1 small zucchini, blanch briefly, combine with 3 tablespoons lemon juice, 1 pinch sugar, and 5 tablespoons oil, and pour over the meat. Top with $1^3/_4$ oz (50 g) capers and 3 tablespoons basil in strips.

Preparation time: 30 minutes

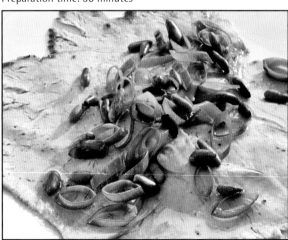

... with turkey breast and roasted pine nuts
Fry 14 oz (400 g) turkey breasts in 2 tablespoons hot olive oil for around 8 minutes each side. Leave to cool. Cut into wafer-thin slices and season with salt and pepper. Arrange on a platter and sprinkle with 2 chopped scallions. Mix together 4 tablespoons orange juice and 2 tablespoons olive oil, then drizzle over the meat. Toast $3^1/_4$ cup (100 g) pine nuts and sprinkle on top.

variations

meat or fish, it's incredibly easy to make. If you prefer, you can also cut cooked meat into thin slices, garnish with cheese, truffles, or pine nuts, and serve alongside a tasty dip.

DIPS
for carpaccio

Creamy dips go equally well with carpaccio. Fresh bread to accompany them is a must.

Preparation time: 20 minutes

... with tuna and lime dressing

Freeze 14 oz (400 g) fresh tuna and cut into wafer-thin slices. Arrange on a platter. Mix together 4 tablespoons lime juice, 3 tablespoons sesame oil, 2 tablespoons fish sauce, salt, and pepper, and $1/4$ teaspoon wasabi, and pour over the fish. Sprinkle with chopped parsley.

Tartare sauce

Mix together chopped boiled eggs, mayonnaise, sour cream, chopped gherkins, chopped herbs, and capers. Perfect with meat carpaccio.

Trout cream

Blend together smoked trout fillet, chopped dill, mustard, lemon juice, salt, and pepper. Perfect with veal and turkey breast.

Preparation time: 20 minutes

... with salmon and horseradish cream

Freeze 14 oz (400 g) fresh salmon, cut into thin slices, and arrange on a platter. Season with salt and pepper and drizzle with lemon juice. Mix together 1 tablespoon freshly grated horseradish and 7 tablespoons (100 ml) heavy whipping cream, stiffly whisked. Use a piping bag to dab the salmon with cream. Sprinkle with chopped dill.

Rémoulade

Combine egg yolk, vinegar, mustard, and oil to make a mayonnaise. Season with freshly chopped herbs, salt, pepper, and lemon juice. Perfect with fish and meat carpaccio.

PANCAKE ROLLS

with spinach and cream cheese

INFO

Spinach is actually not as valuable a food source as it was long thought to be, since its iron levels are clearly overstated. Nevertheless, this green leafy vegetable is still considered a good source of vitamins and minerals. Delicate summer spinach is particularly good eaten raw, while winter spinach, with its stronger flavour, can be blanched for just a short while or tossed in fat until it wilts.

Serves 4

2	*eggs*
5 tbsp	*flour*
	Salt
7 tbsp (100) ml	*milk*
14 oz (400 g)	*spinach*
1 tbsp	*clarified butter*
3¹/₂ oz (100 g)	*cream cheese*
	Pepper
30 min.	*preparation time*

Step by step

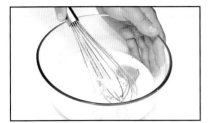

Mix the eggs, flour, a pinch of salt and the milk to form a batter. Leave to stand for 60 minutes.

Sort and wash the spinach, and blanch in boiling water. Drain, squeeze out any remaining liquid and chop.

Use the batter to cook 4 thin pancakes in hot clarified butter. Drain on paper towels.

Spread the pancakes with cream cheese and top with spinach. Season with salt and pepper.

Roll pancakes up and cut diagonally into pieces,

Side dish

To make **salmon tartare**, cut 9 oz (250 g) marinated salmon into small pieces. Combine with 1 finely chopped scallion, 2 tablespoons chopped dill, and $^3/_4$ oz (20 g) chopped, drained capers. Mix the juice of half a lime with $^1/_2$ teaspoon mustard, 5 tablespoons olive oil, salt, pepper, and sugar, and add to the salmon tartare.

Salad

To make **raw celery salad**, peel and finely slice 1-2 celery stalks. Prepare a dressing with generous $^3/_4$ cup (200 ml) vegetable bouillon, 4 tablespoons sherry vinegar, 1 teaspoon ground ginger, 3 tablespoons sunflower oil, salt, pepper, and mix with the celery.

SALADS
to serve with pancakes

These elegantly filled pancake rolls taste even better when accompanied by fresh, crispy salad. The three salads shown here can be eaten with all the recipe variations.

Tomato and scallion salad
Slice some tomatoes and mix with chopped scallions. Drizzle with a dressing made of balsamic vinegar, olive oil, salt, and pepper.

Green bean salad
Mix together cooked green beans, chopped onion, and a dressing made of white wine vinegar, walnut oil, salt, and pepper. Sprinkle with chopped nuts.

Radish and apple salad
Grate white radish and apple. Prepare a dressing using lemon juice, oil, salt, pepper, and sugar, and mix into the salad. Top with halved strawberries.

Preparation time: 30 minutes

... with salmon and sour cream
Prepare the batter and make pancakes as shown on page 28. Divide 9 oz (250 g) marinated salmon into 4 portions. Spread the pancakes with generous $^3/_4$ cup (200 ml) sour cream, sprinkle with chopped chives, and place the salmon on top. Roll the pancakes up and cut into pieces.

Preparation time: 30 minutes

... with asparagus and Parma ham
Prepare the batter and make pancakes as shown on page 28. Mix together 8 tablespoons mayonnaise with 1 tablespoon mustard, and spread over the pancakes. Place $^1/_2$ slice Parma ham and 2–3 boiled and halved asparagus spears on each pancake. Roll them up and cut diagonally into pieces.

PANCAKE ROLLS
several variations

Pancake mix is quick to prepare and the pancakes themselves cook in no time at all.
Put some imagination into fillings, with ham, bacon, cheese, fish, and vegetables.
We've selected and tested six delicious variations.

Preparation time: 30 minutes

... with tuna cream and salad

Prepare the batter and make the pancakes as shown on page 28.
Place 1 green salad leaf on each pancake. Mash 9 oz (250 g)
drained tuna with a fork, combine with mayonnaise, chopped
gherkins, and spread over pancakes. Roll up and cut diagonally
into pieces.

Preparation time: 30 minutes

... with boiled ham and cheese

Prepare and make the pancakes as shown on page 28. Spread
each pancake with 1 tablespoon fig mustard and place 1 slice
boiled ham and 1 slice Gouda on each. Add a few pieces of
tomato, bell pepper, and pickled gherkin to each pancake. Roll
pancakes up and cut diagonally into pieces.

Preparation time: 30 minutes

... with bacon, goat's cheese, and maple syrup

Prepare the batter and make the pancakes as shown on page 28.
Fry 16 bacon rashers until crisp. Place a few arugula leaves,
4 bacon rashers, and 4 slices goat's Camembert on each
pancake. Drizzle with maple syrup. Roll pancakes up and cut
diagonally into pieces.

Preparation time: 30 minutes

... with ewe's milk cheese, tomatoes, and cucumber

Prepare the batter and make the pancakes as shown on page 28.
Crumble 9 oz (250 g) ewe's milk cheese and mix with 4 chopped
sun-dried tomatoes, 10 chopped olives, thyme and rosemary.
Place 1 lettuce leaf on each pancake and add some of the
cheese mixture. Add 4 slices each of cucumber and tomato to
each pancake, roll up, and cut into pieces.

FILLED BAGUETTE
with chicken breast and sala

Serves 4

14 oz (400 g)	*chicken breast fillets*
2 tbsp	*olive oil*
	Salt
	Pepper
	Curry powder
4	*baguettes*
2 tbsp	*butter*
¼ head	*oak leaf lettuce*
6 tbsp (100 g)	*yogurt*
3 tbsp	*mango chutney (see Chutney info)*
25 min.	*preparation time*

Step by step

Wash the chicken fillets, pat dry, and remove the skin and tendons. Heat the oil in a pan.

Wash the lettuce, shake dry, and place some leaves on one half of each baguette.

Fry the chicken for approximately 6 minutes on each side. Season with salt, pepper, and curry powder, and leave to cool.

Slice the chicken breast and place on top of the lettuce.

Slice the baguettes and spread with butter.

Mix together the yogurt and mango chutney and spread over the chicken. Cover with the other half of the baguette.

CURRY INFO

Curry is an Indian dish made with vegetables and meat or fish, plus a sauce. As curry powder, it describes a blend of up to around

40 different spices. While in India the mixture is different for every dish, the blend available here usually contains the same spices; chile, pepper, turmeric, cumin, cardamom, coriander, ginger, and fenugreek.

CHUTNEY INFO

Chutney is used to describe a mix of fruit and sweet vegetables that are cooked and combined with onions, mustard seeds, and strong spices to form a savory dip. To make mango chutney, cook 9 oz

(250 g) diced mango, 5 table-spoons water, 4½ oz (125 g) sugar, 4 tablespoons vinegar, 1 teaspoon salt, ½ teaspoon ground anise, 5 peppercorns, 2 cinnamon sticks, 3 cloves, 2 bay leaves, ½ teaspoon cayenne, and 1 teaspoon ground paprika for approximately 20–30 minutes.

DIPS
for baguettes

Try spreading an aromatic dip on sliced bread or rolls instead of butter.

Orange mayonnaise
Mix the grated rind and juice of 1 organic orange with mayonnaise. Season with chile powder and salt. Perfect with poultry and ham.

Mustard and arugula dip
Blend together arugula, yogurt, mayonnaise, and mustard. Season with salt and pepper. Perfect with salmon and Bündenfleisch.

Herby yogurt dip
Combine olive oil, yogurt, mustard, and vinegar with chopped herbs (chervil, parsley and chives). Perfect with vegetables.

FILLED BAGUETTES
several

There's no need to worry about getting hungry in between meals with these tasty baguettes! Gone are the days of boring sandwiches. Now you can choose between baguettes, flatbreads, bagels, and wholemeal rolls, imaginatively filled with salad, sprouts,

Preparation time: 10 minutes

... with roast beef and vegetables
Make diagonal cuts along the surface of 1 baguette. Spread the cuts with 2 tablespoons herb butter. Finely dice 3$^1/_2$ oz (100 g) zucchini, 1 red bell pepper, and 3$^1/_2$ oz (100 g) roast beef and press the mixture into the cuts. Sprinkle with scant 1 cup (100 g) grated Emmental and bake in the oven at 400 °F/200 °C for 8 minutes.

Preparation time: 15 minutes

... with Bündenfleisch, pear, and cress
Cut 4 wholemeal bread rolls in half and spread with 2 tablespoons herb butter. Cut 7 oz (200 g) chicory into strips, drizzle with lemon juice, and divide between the bottom halves of the rolls. Follow with 5$^1/_2$ oz (150 g) Bündenfleisch slices then place a slice of peeled, cored pear on each. Sprinkle with cress and cover with the top halves of the rolls.

variations

vegetables, fruit, and herbs besides the normal ham, cheese, beef and chicken. Add a tangy dip for an extra treat. These energizing snacks are just the thing, whether you're on the move, at the office, or at a picnic.

Preparation time: 20 minutes

... with Parma ham, Camembert, and peach

Cut 4 bagels in half. Spread the bottom halves with 2 table-spoons butter and place 4 washed leaves of radicchio on top. Add 3$^1/_2$ oz (100 g) Parma ham in thin slices followed by 3 oz (80 g) sliced Camembert. Top with canned peach slices and cover with the other halves of the bagels.

Preparation time: 10 minutes

... with cream cheese, salmon, and radish sprouts

Cut 4 seeded baguettes in half and toast lightly. Spread the bottom halves with 3$^1/_2$ oz (100 g) horseradish cream cheese. Place 5$^1/_2$ oz (150 g) smoked salmon in slices on top of the cream cheese, add radish sprouts, and cover with the other halves of the baguettes.

SPREADS
to serve with baguettes

These spreads can be prepared in an instant and offer extra variety.

Cranberry cream

Mix cranberries from a jar with whisked light whipping cream. Perfect with baguettes filled with Bündenfleisch and Parma ham with Camembert.

Cream cheese spread

Mix cream cheese with paprika, milk, salt, pepper, port, and curry powder. Perfect with all recipe variations.

Egg spread

Mix chopped, hard-boiled egg with finely diced onion, red bell pepper, light cream, crème fraîche, salt, pepper and chopped parsley. Perfect with ham, chicken, and roast beef.

CREAMY SOUP
with tomato and goat's cheese

INFO

Called "paradise apple" in Austria and "golden apple" in Italy, the **tomato** belongs to the nightshade family. When unripe, tomatoes contain a poisonous alkaloid that disappears as the fruit matures. They come in all sorts of shapes, sizes, and colours, ranging from yellow through violet. One particularly striking variety is the huge, wrinkled Bull's Heart. Fresh, canned, pickled or dried–tomatoes are exceptionally versatile.

Serves 4

2¹/₄ lb (1 kg)	aromatic tomatoes (or canned tomatoes)
2	onions
1	clove garlic
2 tbsp	olive oil
2 cups (500 ml)	vegetable bouillon
	Salt
	Pepper
1	egg yolk
3 tbsp	light cream
4¹/₂ oz (125 g)	mature goat's cheese
30 min.	preparation time

Step by step

Score the tomatoes, briefly immerse in boiling water, remove the skin and seeds, then dice.

Peel and chop the onions and garlic. Heat the oil and sweat the onions and garlic until soft.

Add the diced tomatoes and bouillon. Bring to the boil and simmer for 15 minutes.

Purée the soup and season with salt and pepper. Whisk the egg yolk and cream and add to the soup.

Cut the goat's cheese into cubes and sprinkle over the soup.

Side dish

To make **sausage meatballs**, shape 6 oz (175 g) sausage meat into small meatballs with moist hands.

Heat 1 tablespoon olive oil in a pan and fry the meatballs, turning frequently.

Side dish

To make **garlic bread**, cut 1 baguette into slices. Heat 2 tablespoons olive oil in a skillet and sweat 1 finely chopped garlic clove. Add the slices of bread to the pan and fry until crispy and golden brown on both sides.

CREAMY SOUP
several variations

With soups as creamy as those shown here, you can't help but go back for more! Even vegetable sceptics will be impressed by their delicate flavours.

Preparation time: 30 minutes

... with asparagus and ham

Peel generous 1 lb (500 g) white asparagus, cut into pieces, and simmer for 15 minutes with $3^1/_3$ cups (800 ml) vegetable bouillon, salt, sugar, and the juice of half a lemon. Purée the soup and thicken with beurre manié. Simmer for another 5 minutes, then add 3 tablespoons crème fraîche. Warm $5^1/_2$ oz (150 g) boiled ham, cut into strips, in the soup.

Preparation time: 25 minutes

... with fresh herbs and cream

Sweat 1 chopped onion and 1 pressed garlic clove in 1 table-spoon butter. Add 1 cup (250 ml) half-and-half cream and 1 cup (250 ml) chicken bouillon. Simmer for 10 minutes. Add 2 bunches mixed chopped seasonal herbs, and leave to stand for 5 minutes. Combine 1 teaspoon butter with 2 teaspoons all-purpose flour and use to thicken the soup. Garnish with rosettes of stiffly whipped light whipping cream.

Preparation time: 30 minutes

... with zucchini and croutons

Sweat 1 chopped onion, 1 pressed garlic clove and 7 oz (200 g) diced potatoes in 1 tablespoon oil. Add $2^1/_2$ cups (600 ml) chicken bouillon and simmer for 10 minutes. Add generous 1 lb (500 g) zucchini and simmer for 7 minutes. Purée with 2 tablespoons crème fraîche and season with salt and pepper. Sprinkle with 4 tablespoons white bread croutons.

Preparation time: 30 minutes

... with carrot, orange, and ginger

Dice $5^1/_2$ oz (150 g) potatoes, generous 1 lb (500 g) carrots, and 1 onion and sweat in 2 tablespoons oil. Add $3^1/_4$ cups (750 ml) vegetable bouillon and simmer for 20 minutes. Stir in 1 table-spoon grated ginger. Squeeze 3 organic oranges and grate the rind of one of them. Add the juice and zest to the soup. Season with salt, pepper, and chile powder. Stir in generous $3/_4$ cup (200 ml) crème fraîche. Sprinkle with toasted sesame seeds.

SIDE DISHES
to serve with soup

Add extra bite to soups with these crispy treats.

Preparation time: 30 minutes

... with pumpkin and roasted pumpkin seeds

Sweat 2 chopped onions in 2 tablespoons butter. Add 1 tablespoon curry powder, then $2^1/_4$ lb (1 kg) diced pumpkin and $3^1/_4$ cups (750 ml) vegetable bouillon. Simmer for 15 minutes. Purée the soup and season with salt and pepper. Stir 1 egg yolk into generous $^3/_4$ cup (200 ml) light cream and use to thicken the soup. Sprinkle with roasted pumpkin seeds.

Preparation time: 20 minutes

... with herby cream cheese and white wine

Cut 1 bunch scallions into rings and sweat in 2 tablespoons butter. Add 2 cups (500 ml) chicken bouillon and 2 cups (500 ml) milk, and bring to the boil. Add 9 oz (250 g) cream cheese with herbs and dissolve while stirring. Thicken with cornstarch dissolved in water. Add 5 tablespoons white wine and season with salt and pepper. Garnish with cress.

Fried mini dumplings

Work stale bread, milk, light cream, chopped chives, egg yolk, salt, pepper, and nutmeg into a dough. Make 12 dumplings and fry in hot fat. Perfect with asparagus, cheese, and herb soups.

Wholemeal croutons

Cut the crusts from 2 slices wholemeal bread and cube. Heat 2 tablespoons sunflower oil in a pan and brown the pieces of bread until crispy.

Rice balls

Cook sticky rice according to the pack instructions. Make into small balls, roll in breadcrumbs with chopped herbs or grated cheese, and fry in hot fat. Perfect with all recipe variations.

GARLIC INFO

Garlic is something you either love or hate! The scent of essential garlic oil with the active component alliin, responsible for changing the smell of your breath, certainly isn't to everyone's taste. It is, after all, also known as "Stinking Rose." Nevertheless, Mediterranean cuisine would certainly be lacking without it. Just like

onions, garlic belongs to the lily family, even though it sadly lacks the flower's sweet scent. This is down to the sulphur-containing compound found in garlic, alliin which is formed by a chemical reaction which takes place when the bulb is crushed. In spite of all this, garlic is said to have many health benefits. Among other things, it contains various antibiotic substances and is said to inhibit cancer growth.

CIABATTA INFO

The crunchy white bread is an Italian invention that now enjoys great popularity everywhere. The dough used to make **ciabatta** must

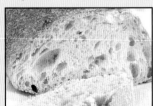

contain olive oil and be oblong in shape. As far as other ingredients such as olives, sun-dried tomatoes or herbs are concerned, these are down to the imagination of the baker. Most importantly, the crust should be light yellow and crisp and the inside light and airy.

Serves 4

4–5	tomatoes
2	onions
1	clove garlic
8 tbsp	balsamic vinegar
5 tbsp	olive oil
	Salt
	Pepper
1	ciabatta loaf
25 min.	preparation time

Step by step

Score the tomatoes crosswise, briefly immerse in boiling water, remove the skins and seeds, and dice.

Heat the ciabatta in the oven at 400 °F/200 °C. Remove and cut into slices.

Peel and finely chop the onions and garlic.

Spread the ciabatta slices with the rest of the olive oil, then toast in a pan.

Mix together the tomatoes, onion, garlic, balsamic vinegar, and 3 tablespoons olive oil. Season with salt and pepper.

Spread the tomato, onion, and garlic mixture over the ciabatta slices.

CROSTINI
with tomatoes and garlic

SPREADS
to serve with crostini

Just because they taste so good and take so little time to prepare, here are another three spreads to serve with slices of toasted bread.

Olive cream
Blend pitted black or green olives, anchovies, capers, lemon juice, and olive oil. Perfect with olive bread.

Sun-dried tomato cream
Blend sun-dried tomatoes with cream cheese and basil. Season with salt, pepper, and balsamic vinegar.

Roquefort cream
Blend Roquefort, pearl onions, chopped walnuts, cornichons, and horseradish. Stir in yogurt and mayonnaise. Season with salt and Tabasco® Sauce.

CROSTINI
several

Crostini is a typical Italian appetizer that, when made in the traditional manner with tomatoes and onions, is also known as "bruschetta." Although the Italians are very good at inventing new toppings for toasted slices of bread, these remain a firm favourite. The four variations shown below are just a small sample

Preparation time: 25 minutes

... with mushroom cream
Sweat $3^1/_2$ oz (100 g) porcini and $3^1/_2$ oz (100 g) mushrooms and 1 chopped onion and garlic clove in 1 tablespoon olive oil. Season with salt, pepper, and thyme. Blend mushrooms and 3 tablespoons parsley. Stir in 3 tablespoons crème fraîche. Toast ciabatta bread and spread with mushroom cream. Sprinkle with Parmesan and grill.

Preparation time: 30 minutes

... with eggplant purée
Pierce 1 eggplant several times and bake in the oven at 480 °F/250 °C for 20 minutes. Remove the skin and blend with 7 tablespoons (100 ml) sour cream, 1 tablespoon sesame paste, salt, pepper, 2 tablespoons olive oil, 2 tablespoons chopped parsley, and 2 tablespoons chopped walnuts. Spread on toasted bread and top with strips of tomato.

variations

of spreads used on crostini. You can add to these to your heart's content. If you like it, and it tastes good, it's allowed. The name "crostino" comes from the Italian word "crostino," which means "little toast."

Preparation time: 25 minutes

... with chicken livers and capers

Fry 7 oz (200 g) chicken livers with chopped onion in hot fat for 3 minutes each side. Add salt, 3 tablespoons white wine, 2 anchovies, and 2 teaspoons capers. Cook for 3 minutes then pulse in a blender with 3 tablespoons chopped parsley. Toast ciabatta slices and spread with chicken liver mixture.

Preparation time: 25 minutes

... with anchovy cream and mozzarella

Blend 4 anchovy fillets with 2 tablespoons drained capers and 2 chopped garlic cloves. Stir in $^1/_2$ bunch chopped parsley and 4 tablespoons olive oil. Season with pepper. Spread 4 pieces of bread with anchovy cream, top with $3^1/_2$ oz (100 g) sliced mozzarella, and bake at 480 °F/250 °C for 5 minutes.

SPREADS
to serve with crostini

If that is still not enough, try these other spreads to go with the bread of your choice.

Cream cheese spread

Mix cream cheese with milk, curry powder, ground paprika, salt, pepper, and chopped cilantro. Perfect with rye bread.

Avocado cream

Blend avocado, chopped chile, lemon juice, yogurt, salt, and pepper. Leave to infuse. Season. Perfect with herb bread.

White bean cream

Sweat cooked white beans in a pan with chopped onion, add some vegetable bouillon, and bring to the boil. Season with salt, cayenne, and lemon juice. Mix with strips of salami. Perfect with herb bread.

OMELET
with mixed vegetables

INFO

Sugar snap peas–also known as sweet peas or mange-tout–can be eaten whole in their pods. With their slightly sweet flavour, the pods are harvested early while still tender and before the formation of any tough skin. When washing them, only the outer fibers need to be removed. Blanched briefly and tossed in butter, sugar snap peas add an elegant touch to vegetable, meat, and fish dishes.

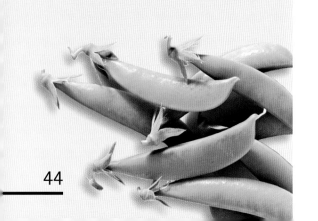

Serves 4

1	*onion*
2	*carrots*
3¹/₂ oz (100 g)	*sugar snap peas*
1 tbsp	*sunflower oil*
3¹/₂ oz (100 g)	*white asparagus from a jar, drained*
8	*eggs*
	Salt
	Pepper
2 tbsp	*chopped parsley*
2 tbsp	*toasted sunflower seeds*
25 min.	*preparation time*

Step by step

Peel and chop the onion. Peel the carrots and dice finely. Wash and finely chop the peas.

Heat the oil in a large omelet pan and sweat the onion until soft.

Add the peas and carrots to the onion and cook while stirring for 5 minutes. Fold in the chopped asparagus.

Whisk the eggs, season with salt and pepper, fold in the parsley, and add the mixture to the vegetables. Leave to set then turn several times.

Roll up the omelet, cut into pieces, and sprinkle with sunflower seeds.

Salad

To make **iceberg and corn salad,** cut the leaves of 1 iceberg lettuce into small pieces. Mix in a bowl with 2 diced red bell peppers, 2 scallions chopped into rings and 3^1/$_2$ oz (100 g) canned sweet corn. Prepare a dressing using 3 tablespoons lemon juice, 6 tablespoons yogurt, salt, pepper, and Worcestershire sauce. Pour over the salad.

Relish

To make **red onion relish**, peel 5^1/$_2$ oz (150 g) red onion and cut into slices. Sprinkle with 1 teaspoon salt in a bowl and leave to stand for 20 minutes. Douse onion with boiling water and drain. Combine 3 tablespoons white wine vinegar, 1 teaspoon lemon juice, and ^{1}/$_4$ teaspoon oregano with the onions.

DIPS
for omelets

Savory dips, relishes, or Indian raitas make a welcoming and refreshing addition to the delicious omelets shown here.

Herb dip
Mix together yogurt, cream cheese, crème fraîche, chopped herbs, celery salt, and pepper. Perfect with mushroom, ewe's milk cheese, and shrimp omelets.

Corn and chile relish
Cook chopped red chile, green bell pepper, and sweet corn for 15 minutes in a mixture of white wine vinegar, sugar, mustard powder, and salt. Perfect with all recipe variations.

Cucumber and tomato raita
Mix peeled and diced cucumber with chopped tomato, yogurt, salt, pepper, curry powder, and ground cumin. Perfect with all recipe variations.

Preparation time: 20 minutes

... with fried chanterelles and herbs
Wash 7 oz (200 g) chanterelles, cut into small pieces, and sauté with 1 chopped onion in 2 tablespoons clarified butter for 5 minutes. Whisk 8 eggs, season with salt, pepper, and $^1/_2$ teaspoon dried thyme, and add to the mushrooms. Leave to set. Sprinkle omelet with 2 tablespoons chopped herbs, cut into pieces and serve.

Preparation time: 20 minutes

... with red onion, garlic, and shrimp
Peel 2 onions, cut into rings, and sweat in an omelet pan with 1 tablespoon oil until soft. Add 2 chopped garlic cloves. Whisk 8 eggs, season with salt and pepper, and pour into the pan. After 1 minute, add $5^1/_2$ oz (150 g) cooked shrimp and leave to set. Sprinkle with chopped dill.

OMELET
several variations

Omelets are quick to prepare and very versatile. Serve hot with cheese or mushrooms, with beans, or as a Spanish omelet with potatoes. And they're just as tasty cold for picnics.

Preparation time: 20 minutes

... with ewe's milk cheese and tomato

Heat 2 sliced tomatoes and 5$^1/_2$ oz (150 g) diced ewe's milk in 1 tablespoon olive oil for 3 minutes. Whisk 8 eggs and season with salt, pepper, and $^1/_2$ teaspoon paprika. Pour over the cheese mixture and cook until set. Sprinkle with chopped olives.

Preparation time: 20 minutes

... with scallions, bell pepper, and cilantro

Sweat 1 chopped onion, 1 diced red bell pepper, and the white part of 3 scallions cut into rings in 2 tablespoons oil for 3 minutes. Whisk 8 eggs, season with salt and pepper, and 1$^1/_2$ teaspoons curry powder. Pour over the vegetables and sprinkle with 3 table-spoons chopped cilantro. Cook until set, roll up, sprinkle with chopped peanuts, and serve.

Preparation time: 30 minutes

... with potato, bacon, and bell pepper

Fry 2$^1/_2$ oz (75 g) diced bacon in 1 tablespoon oil. Add 1 chopped green bell pepper and cook for 3 minutes. Add 7 oz (200 g) boiled and diced potatoes and continue cooking for another 3 minutes. Whisk 6 eggs, season with salt and pepper, and add to the pan. Add 3 tablespoons (25 g) toasted pine nuts and cook until set.

Preparation time: 20 minutes

... with chile, red beans, and cheese

Sweat 1 chopped shallot and $^1/_2$ chopped red chile in 1 table-spoon corn oil for 3 minutes. Add 5$^1/_2$ oz (150 g) canned red beans and cook for another 1 minute. Whisk 8 eggs, season with salt and cayenne, and pour into the omelet pan. After 1 minute, sprinkle with 7 tablespoons (50 g) grated cheese and cook until set. Cut into pieces.

TOASTED SANDWICH
with cheese and ham

Serves 4	
2	eggs
1³/₄ cup (200 g)	grated Emmental
1 tsp	mustard
	Salt
	Pepper
2 drops	Tabasco® Sauce
8 slices	bread for toasting
3 tbsp	butter
4 slices	boiled ham
1	chopped scallion
20 min.	preparation time

Step by step

Mix the eggs with 1¹/₂ cups (175 g) of the cheese, the mustard, salt, pepper, and Tabasco® Sauce.

Place one slice of ham on each followed by the other slice of bread, buttered side up.

Spread one side of each slice of bread with butter.

Sprinkle the sandwiches with the remaining cheese and bake at 400 °F/200 °C for 10 minutes.

Spread the cheese mixture onto 4 slices of the bread.

Sprinkle with chopped scallion and serve.

EMMENTAL INFO

Emmental, with its slightly piquant flavor and famous holes, originates from the Swiss canton of Bern and was originally pro-

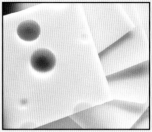

duced as a mountain cheese. Made with raw milk and light yellow in colour, it has a nutty flavour and a fat in dry matter content of around 37 percent. No longer only produced in Switzerland, it is a very versatile cheese that, when grated for example, adds a truly hearty flavor to food.

TABASCO® INFO

Made from chiles, **Tabasco®** is one of the best-known spicy pepper sauces in the world. Just a few drops are enough to add a hot and spicy kick to dishes. Particularly popular in Mexican cuisine, Tabasco® consists of a paste of crushed chile and salt,

to which vinegar is added. Aged in oak barrels, it takes several months for the spicy sauce to mature.

SALADS
for toasted sandwiches

A fresh crisp salad always tastes great alongside the crunchy toasted sandwiches shown here.

Arugula and pear salad
Mix arugula leaves with a dressing of balsamic vinegar, salt, and pepper. Add slices of pear and lemon juice and sprinkle with raisins and toasted pine nuts.

Salad à la niçoise
Mix lettuce, cucumber, bell pepper, tomato, scallions, and olives with red wine dressing. Fold in hard boiled eggs and anchovy fillets.

Radish and celery salad
Mix together radishes, sliced celery, chopped chile, garlic, yogurt, salt, pepper, and olive oil.

TOASTED
several

The sandwich-two slices of white bread with a tasty filling-is a British invention. And, while the British enjoyed cucumber and chicken sandwiches, America invented the club sandwich, consisting of toasted bread, chicken, bacon, salad, and mayonnaise. Meanwhile, popular variations in France are "croque

Preparation time: 20 minutes

... with cured beef, avocado, and Brie
Halve 1 flatbread lengthways, cut into quarters, place the bottom pieces cut side down in a skillet, and fry in 2 tablespoons hot garlic oil. Place 1 slice cured beef and 2 slices avocado on each piece of fried bread and season with salt. Add 3 slices of Brie to each. Bake for 8 minutes at 400 °F/200 °C. Cover with the other half of the bread.

Preparation time: 20 minutes

... with mozzarella, Parma ham and tomatoes
Cut 4 baguettes in half, lightly toast, sprinkle each half with olive oil, and add 1 slice of Parma ham to each. Place 2 sliced tomatoes on top and season with salt. Thinly slice 7 oz (200 g) drained mozzarella, place on top of the tomatoes, and season with pepper. Bake in the oven at 350 °F/180 °C for 8 minutes. Cover with the other half of the bread.

SANDWICHES
variations

monsieur" and "croque madame." These are traditionally made with two slices of white bread filled
with cheese and ham, cooked in a sandwich grilling
iron, and topped with cheese. They resemble the
Italian "tramezzini" with traditional Italian fillings
and toasted white bread.

Preparation time: 20 minutes

... with peaches, goat's cheese, and radicchio

Toast 4 slices of rye bread. Fry 2 peeled and sliced peaches in a
pan with 2 tablespoons butter and season with pepper and sugar.
Place the peaches on the bread and sprinkle with 2 tablespoons
crumbled goat's cheese. Bake at 400 °F/200 °C for 8 minutes. Place
strips of radicchio on top and drizzle with lemon juice and oil.

Preparation time: 30 minutes

... with chicken breast, mango, and cheese

Season 7 oz (200 g) chicken breast fillets with salt and pepper, fry
for 5 minutes in 2 tablespoons oil, and cut into thin slices. Toast
8 pieces of bread and spread each with 1 tablespoon mayonnaise.
Divide the chicken between four slices of toast and top each with
2 pieces of mango. Cover with the other half of the toast topped
with 1 slice Emmental. Bake for 10 minutes at 400 °F/200 °C.

SALADS
for toasted sandwiches

You'll love these three salads to serve alongside
toasted sandwiches.

Apple and cucumber salad

Peel some cucumber and apple, remove the seeds and core,
and slice. Pour over a dressing made from vegetable
bouillon, oil, lemon juice, salt, pepper, and chopped herbs.

Spinach and radicchio salad

Mix spinach with radicchio and diced, fried bacon. Pour over
a dressing made from raspberry vinegar, olive oil, salt, and
pepper. Shave 1³/₄ oz (50 g) Parmesan over the top.

Chinese cabbage salad

Mix together strips of Chinese cabbage with a dressing
made of fish sauce, the zest of a grated lime, the lime juice,
coconut milk, salt, and pepper. Top with sweated shallots,
chile, garlic, and roasted peanuts.

MIXED SALAD
with arugula, nuts, and Parmesan

INFO

Because of its white-veined red leaves, **radicchio** is sometimes also referred to as red-leaf chicory, as it belongs to the same family as the yellow and white bulbs. It is known for its bitter taste, which adds flavor to salads, vegetables, pasta, risotto, and meat dishes. Various types of radicchio are available; the appearance of the leaves, however, whether more elongated or rounded, has no effect on taste.

Serves 4

2	*bunches arugula*
1 head	*radicchio*
1	*red onion*
1	*clove garlic*
3 tbsp	*white wine vinegar*
4 tbsp	*rapeseed oil*
1 tsp	*Dijon mustard*
	Salt
	Pepper
3$^{1}/_{4}$ cup (100 g)	*chopped walnuts*
3$^{1}/_{2}$ oz (100 g)	*Parmesan*
20 min.	*preparation time*

Step by step

Wash the arugula and the radicchio, dry in a salad spinner, remove any hard stems, and tear into small pieces.

Peel and finely chop the onion and garlic. Add to the salad.

Prepare a dressing with the vinegar, oil, mustard, salt, and pepper, and mix into the salad.

Toast the walnuts without any fat and sprinkle into the salad.

Garnish with Parmesan shavings.

Side dish

To make **fried prawns**, wash 12 prawns and remove their shells. Using a sharp knife, cut along the back, remove the black innards, and wash. Heat 3 tablespoons oil in a pan. Add the prawns and fry for approximately 4 minutes, turning frequently.

Dip

To make **aïoli**, use a hand blender to beat 2 eggs, 1 tablespoon vinegar, 1 teaspoon mustard, 1 teaspoon sugar, $^1/_2$ teaspoon salt, and 3 peeled garlic cloves. Add 1 cup (250 ml) rapeseed oil (drop by drop to start with, then as a thin stream) and keep beating to form a creamy mayonnaise. Keep cool until served.

MIXED SALAD
several variations

Fresh, crisp salads taste good at any time of year, whether served as an appetizer or a side dish. There's so much choice that recipes with meat, fish, poultry, cheese, and fruit will ensure variety on your plate week after week.

Preparation time: 30 minutes

... with duck breast and orange slices
Brown 14 oz (400 g) duck breast in 2 tablespoons oil. Brush the skin with honey and bake at 400 °F/200 °C for 8 minutes. Mix slices of orange with $3^1/_2$ oz (100 g) sweet corn, $3^1/_2$ oz (100 g) oak leaf lettuce, and some chopped scallions. Top with a dressing made from 1 tablespoon orange liqueur, 2 tablespoons orange juice, 1 tablespoon vinegar, olive oil, salt, and pepper. Add the duck breast cut into slices.

Preparation time: 25 minutes

... with vegetables and Feta
Cook 11 oz (300 g) shelled fava beans in boiling water for 5 minutes. Combine with $5^1/_2$ oz (150 g) halved cherry tomatoes, 2 chopped garlic cloves, 1 diced yellow bell pepper (all previously sweated in 2 tablespoons oil), 12 pitted black olives, and $4^1/_2$ oz (125 g) diced Feta. Top with a dressing made from 4 tablespoons olive oil, 2 tablespoons white wine vinegar, salt, pepper, and chopped dill.

Preparation time: 25 minutes

... with fried pike perch and sprouts
Toss 11 oz (300 g) mixed sprouts, $^1/_2$ diced cucumber, 1 bunch watercress, and $^1/_2$ bunch sliced radishes in a dressing made from $^1/_2$ cup (125 ml) yogurt, 2 tablespoons lemon juice, 4 tablespoons chopped herbs, salt, and pepper. Season 14 oz (400 g) pike perch fillets with salt and pepper, flour, and fry. Cut into pieces and add to the salad.

Preparation time: 25 minutes

... with mushrooms, Parmesan, and garlic croutons
Wash 1 romaine lettuce, tear the leaves into small pieces, and place in a bowl. Mix together with a dressing made from 1 egg, 1 chopped garlic clove, 2 tablespoons balsamic vinegar, Worcestershire sauce, 4 tablespoons olive oil, salt, and pepper. Wash 9 oz (250 g) mixed mushrooms, and sweat in 2 tablespoons oil with 1 chopped onion for 5 minutes. Fold in the salad. Sprinkle with garlic croutons and Parmesan.

DRESSINGS
for salads

To give the salads additional flavor, we recommend one of the following three delicious dressings:

Gorgonzola and buttermilk dressing
Mix Gorgonzola with mayonnaise, buttermilk, the grated rind and juice of an orange, salt, pepper, and sugar. Perfect with perch pike and cabbage salad.

Filbert dressing
Blend stale white bread (soaked and squeezed) with filberts, chicken bouillon, and garlic. Add olive oil, lemon juice, chives, salt, and pepper. Perfect with cabbage, mushroom, vegetable salad.

Orange and cream dressing
Whisk light whipping cream together with orange juice, sugar, sherry, grated orange rind, salt, and pepper. Perfect with salads containing duck breast and fish.

Preparation time: 25 minutes

... with bacon and goat's cheese baguette
Wash 9 oz (250 g) mixed leaf salad, tear into small pieces, and combine with a dressing made from 4 tablespoons olive oil, 2 tablespoons tarragon vinegar, 2 teaspoons whole grain mustard, 2 tablespoons peanut oil, salt, and pepper. Broil 4 bacon rashers until crisp. Divide 4^1/$_2$ oz (125 g) goat's cheese between 12 baguette slices, broil for 5 minutes, and add to the salad with the bacon.

Preparation time: 25 minutes

... with cabbage, dates, and apple
Cut ^{1}/$_2$ white cabbage and ^{1}/$_2$ red cabbage into thin strips. Chop 1 oz (30 g) pitted dates. Peel, core, and dice 2 apples. Drizzle with lemon juice and add to the cabbage with the dates. Prepare a dressing from 1 teaspoon ground cumin, 4 tablespoons olive oil, 2 tablespoons cider vinegar, 2 tablespoons lemon juice, 1 tablespoon honey, salt, and pepper. Add to the salad.

GAZPACHO INFO

Gazpacho is a soup made of raw vegetables, which is prepared and served cold. Originally from Andalusia, it was introduced by

the Moors who used garlic, cucumber, and bread as their main ingredients.

According to legend, Roman soldiers used a concoction of puréed cucumber, bread, and olive oil to mix with their sour wine.

As tomatoes didn't reach the old world until the arrival of Christopher Columbus, there were no references to them in Spanish cookbooks as an ingredient of gazpacho until the eighteenth century.

The soup is best served ice cold. You can make it spicier by adding chile, leave out the bread to make it thinner, or use croutons instead.

Besides traditional gazpacho there are now a large number of variations, with ingredients ranging from cucumber through beet to pumpkin and melon. The good thing about these soups is that no valuable ingredients are destroyed during the cooking process. They are also low in calories and fat and easy to digest. Even children like them!

Serves 4

1	Spanish onion
3	cloves garlic
1	cucumber
2¼ lb (1 kg)	tomatoes
1	stale bread roll
2 tbsp	vinegar
4 tbsp	olive oil
	Salt
	Pepper
1 each	red and green bell pepper
20 min.	preparation time

Step by step

Peel the onion and garlic cloves. Dice the onion and set half aside.

Blend half the onion, the garlic, half the cucumber, and the tomatoes. Squeeze the excess liquid from the bread roll and blend in.

Peel and dice the cucumber, and set half aside.

Season well with vinegar, oil, salt, and pepper.

Wash and dice the tomatoes. Soak the bread roll in water.

Wash and dice the bell peppers and add to the soup with the remaining diced vegetables.

COLD VEGETABLE SOUP
with bell pepper, tomato, and cucumber

SIDE DISHES
for vegetable soup

Here are a few canapés for those wanting something to nibble with their soup. These can be eaten with all the recipe variations shown here.

Cheese canapés
Spread toasted slices of bread with a topping made from cream cheese, milk, oil, pitted and chopped black olives, diced bell pepper, salt, and pepper, Cut in half before serving.

Salmon canapés
Spread toasted slices of baguette with horseradish cream cheese and top with cucumber and slices of marinated salmon. Sprinkle with dill.

Tartar canapés
Spread toasted, mustard-coated ciabatta slices with cooked ground beef mixed with onions, chile, capers, cucumber, Tabasco® Sauce, salt, and pepper.

COLD VEGETABLE SOUP
several

There's nothing more refreshing to eat on a hot summer's day than cold vegetable soup. You can even have another helping, as it doesn't overload the stomach, contains hardly any calories, and yet is loaded with vitamins and minerals. Here you'll

Preparation time: 20 minutes

... with beets and crème fraîche
Blend 7 oz (200 g) cooked potatoes, 2 diced red onions and $1^3/_4$ lb (800 g) pre-cooked beets. Stir in 3 cups (700 ml) vegetable bouillon. Season with vinegar, salt, pepper and crème fraîche. Garnish with toasted sunflower seeds, whisked light whipping cream, and chopped chives.

Preparation time: 20 minutes

... with almonds and garlic
Blend 7 oz (200 g) shelled almonds, 2 slices soaked and squeezed stale white bread (without the crust), 1 teaspoon salt, and 3 peeled garlic cloves. Add $^2/_3$ cup (150 ml) water, $^2/_3$ cup (150 ml) vegetable bouillon, 4 tablespoons olive oil, and 3 tablespoons sherry vinegar. Season with salt, and pepper. Sprinkle with chopped parsley to serve.

variations

find recipes for four delicious varieties, all of which can be prepared in next to no time. And, if you're still not full, add some little nibbles or skewers with sausage, meat, or vegetables. Try different variations and enjoy the freshness!

Preparation time: 20 minutes

... with cucumber, celery, and cress

Peel and halve 2 lb (900 g) cucumber and remove the seeds. Chop into small pieces with $^1/_2$ stalk celery, and blend with 7 oz (200 g) watercress. Stir in $1^1/_4$ cups (300 ml) milk. Season with 2 tablespoons lemon juice, salt, pepper, olive oil, and Tabasco® Sauce. Sprinkle with chopped dill and serve ice cold.

Preparation time: 20 minutes

... with tomatoes and garlic croutons

Wash and dice $2^1/_4$ lb (1 kg) ripe tomatoes. Blend with 2 onions and 2 garlic cloves. Pass through a sieve. Season with salt, pepper, olive oil, and white balsamic vinegar. Sauté 1 pressed garlic clove in hot oil, add cubes of white bread and fry until crisp. Garnish the soup with shredded basil.

SIDE DISHES
for vegetable soup

Mini skewers are also an extremely tasty addition to cold soups. These can be grilled, or baked, or even served raw.

Sausage and cheese skewers
Alternate cubes of Manchego, chorizo, sun-dried tomatoes, and pitted green olives on soaked wooden skewers.

Chicken and grape skewers
Dice chicken breast fillets, fry in hot oil, season, and alternate on skewers with white and black grape halves.

Grilled vegetable skewers
Alternate common store mushrooms and cubes of zucchini, eggplant, and bell peppers on skewers, brush with oil, and grill for 8 minutes. Season to taste.

PASTA, POTATOES, ETC.

Not only can these dishes be prepared like a flash, they're also very filling and taste delicious.

Here you'll find rice, pasta, and potatoes, all prepared in different ways and all boasting a variety of flavors. There are also vegetables you can cook in a pan or wok in combination with Mediterranean and exotic ingredients, as well as a magical array of spices.

As always, each recipe is shown with a number of variations for you to try out.

PASTA
with ham and cream sauce

INFO

To this day, the question of who invented pasta is still a matter of debate between the Chinese and the Italians. Originally, pasta was made using durum wheat and water. Nowadays, depending on the type of pasta, we add eggs, spices, vegetables, tomatoes, and mushrooms to produce a variety of colors and flavors. Industrially produced pasta is generally made with wheat semolina and eggs, and rarely with spelt.

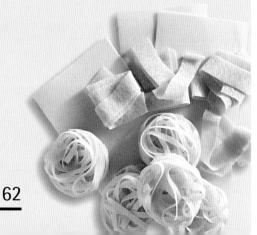

Serves 4

14 oz (400 g)	*spaghetti*
	Salt
5¹/₂ oz (150 g)	*boiled ham*
1	*onion*
1 tbsp	*oil*
3 tbsp	*white wine*
1 cup (250 ml)	*cream*
	Pepper
¹/₂ bunch	*chopped parsley*
20 min.	*preparation time*

Step by step

Cook the spaghetti "al dente" in boiling salt water (about 8–10 minutes).

Dice the ham. Peel the onion and chop finely.

Heat the oil and sweat the onion. Add the wine and boil down a little.

Add the cream and ham to the onion, bring to a boil, and simmer until creamy. Season with salt and pepper.

Strain the pasta and drain well. Serve with the cream and ham sauce and sprinkle with parsley.

Salad

To make **cucumber salad**, peel 1 cucumber and slice thinly. Wash $^1/_2$ bunch dill, shake dry, tear the leaves from the stems, and chop finely. Place the cucumber in a bowl. Prepare a dressing with 3 tablespoons white wine vinegar, $^2/_3$ cup (150 ml) light cream, salt, and pepper, and stir into the cucumber. Fold in the dill.

Salad

To make **mixed salad**, tear the leaves from 2 lettuces into small pieces. Place in a bowl with $^1/_2$ bunch sliced radishes and 4 sliced tomatoes. Prepare a dressing with 1 chopped onion, 3 tablespoons white wine vinegar, 3 tablespoons sunflower oil, salt, pepper, and add to the salad.

PASTA
several variations

What's not to love about delicious pasta in all its different shapes, sizes, and colors? Spaghetti, fusilli, penne, macaroni, and tagliatelle are just a few of the varieties used in cooking. Much more important, however, are the sauces served with them, as shown in the variations below.

Preparation time: 25 minutes

... with venison and mushrooms

Cook 14 oz (400 g) pasta. Fry 20 sage leaves in 1 tablespoon butter. Fry 5^1/$_2$ (150 g) venison fillet, cut into strips, in the butter for 2 minutes. Fry 1 diced onion and 7 oz (200 g) mixed mushrooms in 2 tablespoons clarified butter, season with salt and pepper, and add balsamic vinegar and 2 tablespoons meat bouillon. Add 7 tablespoons (100 ml) light cream, followed by the meat. Fold in the pasta.

Preparation time: 25 minutes

... with green spring vegetables

Cook 14 oz (400 g) fusilli. Blanch 4^1/$_2$ oz (125 g) broccoli florets, 3^1/$_2$ oz (100 g) sugar snap peas, 8 oz (225 g) green asparagus, cut into pieces, 3^1/$_2$ oz (100 g) green garden peas, and 1 diced fennel in boiling, salted water for 5 minutes and drain. Sweat 1 chopped shallot in 1 tablespoon butter. Stir in 1^1/$_4$ cups (300 ml) crème fraîche and 3 tablespoons chopped herbs. Combine with the fusilli and vegetables, and sprinkle with Parmesan.

Preparation time: 20 minutes

... with shrimp and cherry tomatoes

Cook 14 oz (400 g) spaghetti. Sweat 2 chopped garlic cloves in 2 tablespoons olive oil and add generous 1 lb (500 g) halved cherry tomatoes. Season with salt and cayenne. Add the cooked pasta with 7 oz (200 g) shrimp, previously fried in 2 tablespoons olive oil. Sprinkle with parsley, basil, and 3 tablespoons grated Parmesan.

Preparation time: 20 minutes

... with salmon and cream sauce

Cook 14 oz (400 g) green tagliatelle. Sweat 1 chopped shallot in 1 tablespoon olive oil. Add 7 tablespoons (100 ml) white wine and generous ^{3}/$_4$ cup (200 ml) light cream and simmer for 5 minutes. Cut 9 oz (250 g) salmon fillet into pieces and poach in the sauce for 3 minutes. Strain the pasta and serve with the salmon and cream sauce. Sprinkle with chopped dill.

SALADS
for pasta dishes

Our tasty pasta dishes go wonderfully with fresh, crisp salads.

Preparation time: 25 minutes

... with goat's cheese and arugula

Cook 14 oz (400 g) whole wheat pasta. Slice 1 red onion, chop 1 clove garlic, and sweat in 1 tablespoon oil until soft. Add 3$^1/_2$ oz (100 g) soft goat's cheese and cook for 2 minutes. Add $^3/_4$ bunch chopped arugula and continue to simmer. Fold in the drained pasta. Sprinkle with pepper and grated Parmesan.

Preparation time: 30 minutes

... with morels and truffle oil

Cook 14 oz (400 g) fettuccine. Soak 9 oz (250 g) dried morels for 5 minutes, rinse and drain, and cut into quarters. Sweat the mushrooms in 3 tablespoons butter for about 10 minutes, pour in 1 cup (250 ml) light cream and 1 tablespoon sherry, and simmer until creamy. Season with salt, pepper, and lemon juice.
Fold drained pasta into the mushrooms. Sprinkle with truffle oil.

Frisée and carrot salad

Mix frisée leaves, grated carrot, and mandarin segments. Drizzle with a honey dressing and top with fried bacon pieces.

Apple and bell pepper salad

Dice apple, yellow bell pepper, and cucumber. Mix well and drizzle with quark and lemon dressing. Top with onions cut into rings.

Tomato and croutons

Combine 14 oz (400 g) diced tomatoes and chopped scallions with a dressing of balsamic vinegar, olive oil, salt, and pepper. Fold in toasted garlic croutons.

65

PASTA
with pesto

	Serves 4
14 oz (400 g)	spaghetti
	Salt
1 bunch	basil
3	cloves garlic
5 tbsp	pine nuts
1/2 cup (125 ml)	olive oil
2 1/2 oz (75 g)	freshly grated Parmesan
20 min.	preparation time

Step by step

Cook the spaghetti "al dente" in boiling salt water (about 8–10 minutes).

Purée the basil, garlic, and pine nuts in a blender.

Wash the basil and strip the leaves from the stems. Peel the garlic.

Add the oil and Parmesan and work to a smooth paste.

Toast the pine nuts in a skillet without any fat and leave to cool.

Drain the spaghetti well. Warm in a pan with the pesto.

PINE NUTS INFO

Long, pale yellow, and flavorful, **pine nuts** are the edible seeds of pine trees, formed inside the cones. Despite being popular,

they are rather rare and expensive due to the fact that the cones and kernels are only formed every three years. Very high in fat and protein, pine nuts are an essential ingredient of pesto and are often used to enrich fish, meat, and poultry fillings as well as for sprinkling over vegetable dishes. One particularly special ingredient is pine nut oil.

OLIVE OIL INFO

Olive oil is a mainstay of Mediterranean cuisine and, indeed, of anywhere else where healthy cooking is popular. Generally speaking, there are three different flavors: light oils, oils with a medium-fruity aroma, and oils with an intensely fruity aroma,

which tend to be slightly bitterer. Only high quality, cold-pressed oil from the first pressing (extra virgin) should be used for salads and pesto. Organic is the best type of olive oil to use.

67

SAUCES
for pasta dishes

When time is of the essence, try these pasta sauces. They can even be prepared in advance.

Wild garlic pesto
Purée wild garlic leaves, pine nuts, Parmesan, olive oil, and salt in a blender.

Almond and parsley pesto
Blend flat-leaf parsley, basil, garlic, almonds, chile, Parmesan, and olive oil.

Tuna pesto
Blend basil, garlic, pine nuts, and Parmesan. Add olive oil, chopped tomatoes, and drained tuna from a can.

PASTA
several

Pasta is often served as an appetizer in Italy, as all it needs is a little butter and Parmesan, pesto, or garlic and oil. Italy would not be the land of pasta, however, if it weren't for its refined pasta dishes containing fish, other seafood, or meat. When cooking pasta, it is important to serve it "al dente"-"to the bite." This

Preparation time: 15 minutes

... with garlic and oil
Cook 14 oz (400 g) spaghetti "al dente." Peel 4 garlic cloves and shave thinly. Clean, pit, and wash 1 red chile, cut it into rings, and sweat in 6 tablespoons hot olive oil. Sweat the garlic without letting it turn brown. Strain the spaghetti, drain well, and toss in the seasoned oil.

Preparation time: 15 minutes

... with butter and Parmesan
Cook 14 oz (400 g) rigatoni "al dente" in boiling salt water. Grate 3^1/$_2$ oz (100 g) Parmesan. Melt ^{2}/$_3$ cup (150 g) butter and keep stirring until it turns light brown. Fry 10 sage leaves in the butter until crisp. Remove and drain. Strain the pasta, drain well, and mix with the butter. Sprinkle with cheese and serve with sage.

SAUCES
for pasta dishes

means the pasta must not be too soft, but just firm enough to absorb the sauce accompanying it. Cooking with oil should also be avoided, as this prevents the pasta from absorbing other liquids.

Here are three more sauces that taste delicious when teamed with any kind of pasta!

Preparation time: 20 minutes

... with red pesto

Cook 14 oz (400 g) tagliatelle "al dente." Soak $3^1/_2$ oz (100 g) sun-dried tomatoes in $^2/_3$ cup (150 ml) just-boiled water. Leave to stand for 10 minutes, drain, and blend with $1^3/_4$ oz (50 g) toasted walnuts, $1^3/_4$ (50 g) pine nuts, and $^2/_3$ cup (75 g) grated Parmesan. Season with pepper, sugar, and vinegar. Fold in chopped basil and mix with the pasta.

Preparation time: 25 minutes

... with spinach and chile

Cook 14 oz (400 g) macaroni "al dente." Heat 3 tablespoons olive oil and sweat 1 diced red chile, 1 chopped onion, and 1 clove garlic. Add 6 tablespoons (50 g) sesame seeds. Add 9 oz (250 g) washed, young spinach leaves and stir until wilted. Season with pepper and nutmeg. Fold in the drained pasta and shave Parmesan over the top.

Bell pepper sauce

Purée Ricotta, chopped bell pepper, chile, scallions, dill, lemon juice, bouillon, salt, and pepper in a blender.

Broccoli sauce

Blend cooked broccoli, chopped onion, crème fraîche, olive oil, almonds, capers, and lemon juice.

Olive sauce

Blend pitted green olives, marinated anchovies, garlic, olive oil, lemon juice, cognac, salt, and pepper.

RISOTTO
with peas ("risi e bisi")

INFO

Traditional **risotto rice** is a high quality, round-grain rice. The main varieties used in Italy for making risotto are Arborio, Carnaroli, Baldo, and Vialone. Good risotto rice should be very creamy, due to a high starch content, and firm, both before and after cooking. Traditional recipes advise adding the liquid gradually, so the rice can absorb it slowly.

Serves 4	
2	onions
2 tbsp	butter
2 cups (400 g)	risotto rice
4 cups (1 l)	vegetable bouillon
11 oz (300 g)	frozen peas
7 tbsp (100 ml)	light cream
1 bunch	chopped parsley
	Salt
	Pepper
7 tbsp (50 g)	Parmesan
30 min.	preparation time

Step by step

Peel the onions and chop finely. Sweat briefly in the butter.

Add the rice, pour in 1¹/₂ cups (350 ml) vegetable bouillon, and bring to a boil.

Add the frozen peas and simmer for 1 minute.

Pour in the rest of the bouillon and bring back to a boil. Reduce the heat, cover, and simmer for 15 minutes.

Fold in the cream and parsley. Season with salt and pepper, and garnish with shaved Parmesan.

Salad

To make **green salad with raspberry dressing,** clean, wash, dry (in a salad spinner), and tear into small pieces ¹/₄ head each frisée, oak leaf lettuce, and iceberg lettuce, and 3¹/₂ oz (100 g) drained, canned sweet corn.

Fold in 3¹/₂ oz (100 g) sliced mushrooms and ¹/₂ bunch chopped scallions. Toss in a dressing of 3 tablespoons raspberry vinegar, 1 teaspoon mild honey, 1 teaspoon mustard, 4 tablespoons rapeseed oil, salt, and pepper.

Side dish

Fried bacon: Cut 7 oz (200 g) bacon rashers into pieces and fry in a skillet with 1 tablespoon oil until crisp. Scatter over the "risi e bisi."

SIDE DISHES
several variations

Risotto is delicious eaten with crisp fried meat, fish, and poultry.

Fried chicken drumsticks
Rub chicken drumsticks with salt, pepper, and ground paprika, and brown in a pan or in the oven with 3 table-spoons oil. Cover and cook for 20 minutes.

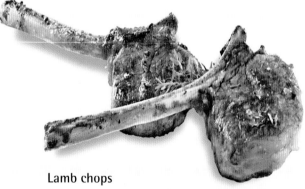

Lamb chops
Season lamb chops with salt, pepper, and thyme and fry in hot olive oil for about 3 minutes each side.

Fried sardines
Rub sardines on both sides with salt and pepper. Fry in hot oil for 2 minutes each side. Sprinkle with chopped parsley.

Preparation time: 30 minutes

... with radicchio and Parmesan
Sweat 1 diced onion and 11 oz (300 g) radicchio, cut into strips, in 2 tablespoons butter and 2 tablespoons olive oil. Add generous ³/₄ cup (200 ml) milk, then 2 cups (400 g) risotto rice. Gradually pour in around 4 cups (1 l) vegetable bouillon, until the rice is creamy. Season with salt and pepper. Fold in 7 tablespoons (50 g) grated Parmesan.

Preparation time: 30 minutes

... with saffron and butter
Sweat 1 peeled and chopped onion with 1 oz (30 g) diced bone marrow in 2 tablespoons butter. Pour in 3 tablespoons red wine and boil down. Add 2 cups (400 g) risotto rice and simmer, gradually pouring in around 4 cups (1 l) chicken bouillon until the rice is creamy. Dissolve 1 sachet saffron in a little water and add to the rice. Fold in 3 tablespoons butter and grated Parmesan.

RISOTTO
several variations

Risotto can be served as a main dish or, alternatively, as a side dish with fish, meat, or poultry. More importantly, once cooked the rice should be creamy and smooth. It should stick to the spoon, not drown in liquid. Risotto can be prepared with a variety of different ingredients.

Preparation time: 30 minutes

... with bolete mushrooms

Chop 9 oz (250 g) soaked bolete and sweat with 1 chopped onion in 2 tablespoons butter. Add 2 cups (400 g) risotto rice. Gradually pour in 3$^1/_3$ cups (800 ml) chicken bouillon and 7 tablespoons (100 ml) white wine, and cook until the rice is creamy. Season and fold in 7 tablespoons (50 g) grated Parmesan and 1 tablespoon butter.

Preparation time: 30 minutes

... with fennel

Clean 14 oz (400 g) fennel, remove the hard outer leaves, and cut into small cubes. Sweat with 1 peeled and chopped onion in 2 tablespoons butter. Add 2 cups (400 g) risotto rice and gradually pour in 3$^1/_4$ cups (750 ml) vegetable bouillon and 1 cup (250 ml) white wine, cooking until the rice is creamy. Season with salt and pepper, and fold in 1 tablespoon butter and grated Parmesan.

Preparation time: 30 minutes

... with pumpkin

Dice 14 oz (400 g) pumpkin. Sweat 2 oz (50 g) diced, smoked bacon with 1 chopped onion and garlic clove in 2 tablespoons olive oil. Add 2 cups (400 g) risotto rice and gradually pour in 4 cups (1 l) fish bouillon, cooking until the rice is creamy. Season and fold in chopped parsley and 7 tablespoons (50 g) Parmesan.

Preparation time: 30 minutes

... with white and green asparagus

Peel the stalks of 9 oz (250 g) each white and green asparagus. Blanch the whole asparagus for 5 minutes in 3$^1/_4$ cups (750 ml) boiling salt water. Drain, reserving the cooking water. Cut off the asparagus tips. Chop the stalks and sweat with 1 chopped onion in 1 tablespoon butter. Add 2 cups (400 g) risotto rice and gradually add the asparagus water and 1 cup (250 ml) white wine, cooking until the rice is creamy. Fold in the asparagus tips, 2 tablespoons butter, and Parmesan.

ZUCCHINI INFO

Like cucumber, **zucchini** belongs to the Cucurbitaceae family. It tastes best when still green (unripe) and no more than

7 in. (17 cm) long, as this is when the flesh is still juicy and crisp. Not only good sautéed in olive oil and served as a side dish, zucchini is delicious as a typical Italian "antipasto," marinated in wine and lemon juice (see page 76). The singular of zucchini is actually zucchino, although it is more usual to refer to it in the plural.

HERBES DE PROVENCE INFO

The term **"herbes de Provence"** is used to describe a mixture of herbs that are typical of France and grow wild in Provence. The main seven herbs used are rose-

mary, thyme, oregano, lavender, bay leaf, sage, and winter savory. Available to buy dried, herbes de Provence is used to season Mediterranean food such as ratatouille and other meat and fish dishes. It can also be used to enrich spiced vinegar and oil.

Serves 4

2	*small zucchini*
2	*red bell peppers*
2	*red onions*
1	*clove garlic*
2 tbsp	*olive oil*
²/₃ cup (150 ml)	*vegetable bouillon*
14 oz (400 g)	*cooked rice (uncooked: 1 cup/200 g)*
	Salt
	Pepper
1 tbsp	*herbes de Provence*
³/₄ cup (100 g)	*pine nuts*
20 min.	*preparation time*

Step by step

Wash, dry, and dice the zucchini. Wash, halve, and deseed the bell peppers. Dice the flesh.

Pour in the vegetable bouillon and continue cooking for 5 minutes.

Peel the onions and garlic and chop finely.

Fold in the rice and cook for a further 5 minutes.

Heat the oil and sweat the onion until soft. Add the garlic and vegetables and simmer for 3 minutes.

Season with salt, pepper, and herbes de Provence, and sprinkle with toasted pine nuts.

FRIED RICE
with zucchini and bell pepper

SIDE DISHES
for fried rice

Try serving marinated vegetables as an accompaniment to rice dishes. They can be prepared in advance and also taste great served cold.

Marinated zucchini

Wash and pat dry 1 lb (500 g) zucchini and cut into thin slices. Sauté in 3 tablespoons olive oil until golden brown on both sides. Season with salt and pepper. Place in a dish. Add the frying juices, the juice of 1 lemon, and 7 tablespoons (100 ml) white wine. Sprinkle with chopped mint and marinate overnight.

Marinated eggplant

Wash and pat dry 1 lb (500 g) eggplant and cut lengthways into thin slices. Place in an ovenproof dish with 5 peeled garlic cloves and season with salt and pepper. Add 5 tablespoons olive oil. Bake in the oven at 400 °F/200 °C for 25 minutes.

FRIED RICE
several

These dishes are ideal for using pre-cooked rice, which can be prepared the day before. Let your imagination run wild and spice things up with vegetables, meat, poultry, or fish. For extra variety,

Preparation time: 20 minutes

... with ground meat and mixed vegetables

Fry 9 oz (250 g) ground meat with 1 chopped onion in 1 tablespoon clarified butter. Season with salt, pepper, and paprika. Brown 1 cup (200 g) cooked rice in 1 tablespoon clarified butter. Add 11 oz (300 g) thawed frozen mixed vegetables (cauliflower, carrots, cut green beans) and the ground meat, and fry for 3 minutes. Add 5 tablespoons bouillon. Season with salt and pepper.

Preparation time: 20 minutes

... with turkey, almonds, and raisins

Sweat 1 diced onion in 2 tablespoons clarified butter until soft. Add 14 oz (400 g) turkey, cut into strips, and continue cooking. Season with 2 tablespoons curry powder. Stir in generous 3$\frac{1}{4}$ cup (100 g) chopped almonds and 3 tablespoons golden raisins, bring to a boil, and season with salt and pepper. Stir in 1$\frac{1}{4}$ cups (250 g) cooked rice and simmer for a further 3 minutes. Fold in 2 tablespoons coconut flakes.

SIDE DISHES
for fried rice

Besides tasting great with fried rice, marinated mushrooms and onions make an ideal appetizer.

Marinated mushrooms

Clean a mixture of generous 1 lb (500 g) common store mushrooms and bolete with a damp cloth. Fry in 3 tablespoons olive oil for 3 minutes. Add the juice and grated rind of 1 lemon, 5 tablespoons white wine, 2 chopped garlic cloves, and $1/_2$ bunch thyme. Sweat for a further 3 minutes and season with salt and pepper. Marinate overnight.

Marinated onions

Brown generous 1 lb (500 g) peeled pearl onions or small shallots in 3 tablespoons olive oil. Add the juice of 1 lemon, $1/_2$ cup (125 ml) white wine, and 20 small sage leaves cut into strips. Cover and simmer for about 4 minutes then season with salt and pepper. Marinate overnight.

variations

try replacing rice with other grains such as millet or bulgur. An advantage of bulgur is that it can be bought pre-cooked and only has to be covered with boiling water and soaked for around 15 minutes.

Preparation time: 15 minutes

... with wok vegetables

Dice 2 carrots. Sweat $3^1/_2$ oz (100 g) sugar snap peas, $3^1/_2$ oz (100 g) broccoli florets, and 1 chopped stalk celery in a wok in 2 tablespoons peanut oil for 3 minutes. Season with salt, pepper, 1 tablespoon soy sauce, and 1 tablespoon fish sauce. Mix in $1^1/_4$ cups (250 g) cooked rice and continue cooking for 2 minutes. Sprinkle with 7 tablespoons (50 g) roasted, chopped peanuts.

Preparation time: 20 minutes

... with Chinese mushrooms and ginger

Chop 1 clove garlic and $1/_2$ in. (1 cm) fresh ginger. Sweat in 1 tablespoon oil and add $3^1/_2$ oz (100 g) frozen peas and $1/_2$ bunch sliced radishes. Add $3^1/_2$ oz (100 g) Chinese mushrooms (soaked for 5 minutes in hot water) including liquid, 1 tablespoon soy sauce, 2 tablespoons bouillon, 1 teaspoon cayenne, and $1^1/_2$ cups (300 g) cooked rice. Cook for 3 minutes. Stir in $1^1/_4$ oz (50 g) watercress and 1 teaspoon sesame seeds.

PAN-COOKED VEGETABLES
with almonds

INFO

Almonds are a tasty treat that aren't used enough in cooking. Eating them reduces the risk of heart disease, as their healthy fats lower cholesterol. The ripe fruit of the almond tree, which is widely cultivated in the Mediterranean, Southern Europe, and North Africa, has a pale kernel surrounded by a thin brown covering and a tan-color shell. Almonds can be sweet, bitter, and soft shelled. Bitter almonds contain amygdalin—a substance that breaks down into hydrocyanic acid, which is toxic to humans.

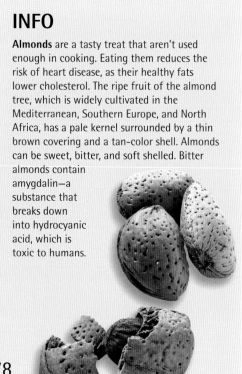

Serves 4

2 each	red and yellow bell peppers
1	Spanish onion
4 tbsp	safflower oil
1 tbsp	chile oil
3$^{1}/_{2}$ oz (100 g)	almonds
1 lb (500 g)	canned plum tomatoes
3 tbsp	wine vinegar
1	orange (juice of)
	Salt
1 bunch	basil, cut into strips
25 min.	preparation time

Step by step

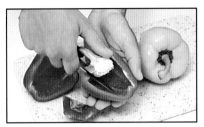

Clean, halve, and deseed the bell peppers.

Peel the onion. Cut the onion and bell peppers into 1-in. (2.4-cm) cubes.

Heat the oils and toast the almonds until golden brown. Add the onion and sweat until soft.

Add the bell peppers and sweat for 1 minute. Then stir in the tomatoes with their juice, the vinegar, and the orange juice.

Simmer for 10 minutes. Season with salt and sprinkle with the basil.

Side dish

To make **garlic bread**, slice 1 baguette and toast. Brush slices with 2 peeled and finely chopped garlic cloves and 3 tablespoons herb butter.

Side dish

To make **polenta pieces**, boil 3¹/₄ cups (750 ml) salt water and gradually add 1³/₄ (250 g) cornmeal. Stir until there are no lumps. Leave the polenta to soak for about 20 minutes while stirring, until the mixture is so thick the spoon stands up in it. Flatten on a floured surface and cut into pieces. Fry the polenta pieces in hot butter until golden brown and serve immediately.

PAN-COOKED VEGETABLES
several variations

Health officials recommend that we eat at least five portions of fruit and vegetables every day. That's no problem—we have more than enough dishes with vegetables here! Try to use seasonal and organic vegetables in your vegetable dishes.

Preparation time: 20 minutes

... with bell pepper and beef strips
Brown 9 oz (250 g) beef, cut into strips, in 4 tablespoons oil. Remove. Sweat chopped ginger and garlic, add 1 yellow and 1 red bell pepper, cut into strips, and fry for 3 minutes. Add meat to vegetables and stir in 2 tablespoons oyster sauce and 1 teaspoon sesame oil. Season with salt and pepper.

Preparation time: 20 minutes

... with bok choy, sprouts, and shrimp
Cut 1 bok choy into strips. Fry 9 oz (250 g) shrimp in 2 tablespoons chile oil for 4 minutes. Remove. Sweat 1 chopped onion, 1 pressed garlic clove, and 1/2 chopped red chile in cooking oil, add the bok choy, and simmer for 2 minutes. Add 7 tablespoons (100 ml) bouillon and simmer for 2 minutes. Stir in 1 3/4 oz (50 g) sprouts and the shrimp. Simmer for another 2 minutes and season.

Preparation time: 20 minutes

... with cellophane noodles, sugar snap peas and carrots
Soak 9 oz (250 g) cellophane noodles in 2 cups (500 ml) hot water for 10 minutes. Cut 3 1/2 oz (100 g) sugar snap peas diagonally and slice 4 carrots. Sweat with chopped ginger in 3 tablespoons. Add 9 oz (250 g) blanched cauliflower florets and 2/3 cup (150 ml) bouillon. Season with salt and pepper and stir in the drained noodles.

Preparation time: 25 minutes

... with white cabbage, ground meat, and onions
Peel 14 oz (400 g) potatoes, season, and cook in salt water for 15 minutes. Fry 9 oz (250 g) ground meat and chopped onion in 2 tablespoons oil until crumbly. Add 11 oz (300 g) white cabbage, cut into strips, pour in generous 3/4 cup (200 ml) bouillon, and cook for 8 minutes. Add the strained potatoes. Season with salt, pepper, and cumin. Sprinkle with chopped parsley.

Preparation time: 20 minutes

... with broccoli, mushrooms, and zucchini

Blanch 9 oz (250 g) broccoli florets for 5 minutes. Dice 2 small zucchini. Sweat with 1 chopped onion in 2 tablespoons oil. Add 4¹/₂ oz (125 g) sliced oyster mushrooms and cook for 3 minutes. Add the broccoli and 4 diced tomatoes. Pour in 3 tablespoons white wine and 7 tablespoons (100 ml) bouillon. Bring to a boil and season. Sprinkle with sesame seeds.

Preparation time: 20 minutes

... with leek, nuts, and tofu

Dice 7 oz (200 g) tofu and marinate in soy sauce and sesame oil for 15 minutes. Cut 2 leeks into rings. Dice 1 yellow bell pepper. Fry the drained tofu in oil until crisp. Remove. Sweat 1 chopped onion, add the leek and bell pepper, and fry for 5 minutes. Stir in 2 tablespoons roasted cashews and the tofu. Add the marinade and season with salt and pepper.

SIDE DISHES
for vegetables

Vegetables can be served with bread, pasta, potatoes, cereals, or rice. Here, we've gone for cereal and rice dishes.

Couscous

Sweat 1¹/₄ cups (250 g) couscous in butter. Add 2 cups (500 ml) vegetable bouillon and cook for 15 minutes. Season with salt and pepper. Add some chopped parsley.

Djuvec rice

Cook 1¹/₄ cups (250 g) parboiled rice in 2 cups (500 ml) water until absorbed. Sweat diced tomatoes in oil. Mix with the rice and season with salt, pepper, and ground paprika.

Cilantro rice

Cook 1¹/₄ cups (250 g) long-grain rice in 2 cups (500 ml) bouillon for about 20 minutes. Add ¹/₂ bunch chopped cilantro.

QUICK PIZZA
with tomato and mozzarella

	Serves 4
1–2	*ready-made pizza dough*
4 tbsp	*oil*
2	*cloves garlic*
1 can	*chopped tomatoes*
	Salt
	Pepper
¹/₂ bunch	*thyme, finely chopped*
6	*beefsteak tomatoes*
14 oz (400 g)	*mozzarella (drained weight)*
¹/₂ bunch	*basil*
30 min.	*Preparation time*

Step by step

Roll out the pizza dough and place on a baking sheet brushed with 1 tablespoon oil.

Remove the stalks from the beef tomatoes and cut into slices. Slice the mozzarella.

Peel and chop the garlic and mix with 2 tablespoons of oil. Use to brush the pizza dough.

Arrange the sliced tomatoes and mozzarella on the pizza. Add salt to the tomatoes. Sprinkle with 1 tablespoon of oil.

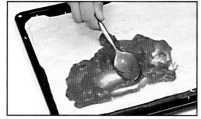

Spread the canned tomatoes over the dough. Season with salt and pepper and sprinkle with thyme.

Bake in the oven at 400 °F/200 °C for about 20 minutes. Garnish with basil.

MOZZARELLA INFO

Real **buffalo mozzarella** (mozzarella di bufala) is made from the milk of water buffalo and is pure white. Boiled and soaked in salt water, it can also be bought in Italy as small balls (occhi di bufala) or plaited (trecce di

mozzarella). With its slightly sour, intense aroma, buffalo mozzarella tastes very fresh, even sweet, and food connoisseurs swear by it. In comparison, the widely available cow's milk variety has less flavor and is more of a yellowish color. Mozzarella has a firm, slightly rubbery consistency, making it ideal for cooking au gratin.

BASIL INFO

The "king of herbs" (from the Greek word basileus = king), **basil** is originally from Italy. Its highly aromatic flavor makes it

the perfect addition to tomato and other vegetable dishes, soups, and salads. It is also an essential ingredient of pesto, a green sauce made with garlic and pine nuts and eaten with pasta. There are a number of different varieties of basil, including some that are red and Thai basil with its small leaves. Basil leaves should always be picked from the top, to encourage growth.

TOPPINGS
for quick pizzas

Try one of these toppings for a delicious, speedy pizza.

Neapolitan style with anchovies
Cover the base with tomato sauce, anchovies, and mozzarella. Season with oregano.

With salami and olives
Cover the base with tomato sauce, sliced salami, olives, and chile.

With clams
Cover the base with tomato sauce, cooked clams, garlic, oregano, and olive oil.

QUICK PIZZA
several

Home-made pizza is always better than ready to cook pizza. Why not invite some friends over for pizza and red wine and all add your own toppings together? Don't worry about making the dough. There's no need to mix yeast dough, leave it to rise,

Preparation time: 30 minutes

... with Serrano ham and Gorgonzola
Place the pizza dough on a greased baking sheet and cover with chopped canned tomatoes. Tear 5 $\frac{1}{2}$ oz (150 g) Serrano ham (if unavailable, use Parma ham) into pieces and spread over the tomatoes. Thinly slice 2 zucchini and arrange on top. Crumble 7 oz (200 g) Gorgonzola over the ham. Bake at 400 °F/200 °C for 20 minutes.

Preparation time: 30 minutes

... with artichokes and olives
Place the pizza dough on a greased baking sheet. Spread with a thin layer of herbed cream cheese. Drain 14 oz (400 g) artichoke hearts from a jar, halve, and spread over the base with 3$\frac{1}{2}$ oz (100 g) sliced mushrooms. Top with 1$\frac{3}{4}$ oz (50 g) halved black olives and drizzle with 2 tablespoons olive oil. Bake in the oven at 400 °F/200 °C for 20 minutes.

TOPPINGS
for quick pizzas

and knead it when you can buy it ready-made from the supermarket. You could try a different kind of ready-made dough, such as puff pastry—great for making a quick pizza at home.

Here are another three suggestions for pizza toppings. Try inventing some more yourself!

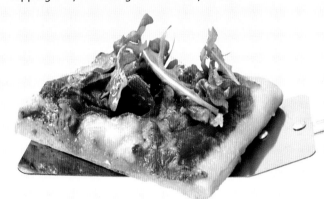

Preparation time: 30 minutes

... with goat's cheese, pears, and honey

Place the pizza dough on a greased baking sheet and brush with generous $^3/_4$ cup (200 ml) crème fraîche. Season with herb salt and pepper. Peel and core 2–3 pears, cut into slices. Spread over the base with 2 sliced rolls of goat's milk cheese. Drizzle with 3 tablespoons honey and bake at 400 °F/200 °C for 20 minutes.

With arugula and Parma ham

Cover the pizza base with tomato sauce, Parma ham cut into strips, and grated cheese. Top with arugula after cooking.

Preparation time: 30 minutes

... with tuna and onions

Place the pizza dough on a greased baking sheet. Brush with $^2/_3$ cup (150 ml) soured cream. Drain 14 oz (400 g) canned tuna and mash with a fork. Spread over the top. Peel 1 Spanish onion, cut into very thin rings, and spread over the tuna. Sprinkle with freshly chopped oregano and bake in the oven at 400 °F/200 °C for 20 minutes.

With ewe's milk cheese and bell pepper

Cover the pizza base with tomato sauce, bell pepper cut into strips, onion rings, and cubes of ewe's milk cheese. Season with thyme and oregano.

With four cheeses (quattro formaggi)

Cover the pizza base with tomato sauce. Top with Provolone, Emmental, Gruyère, and pecorino, grated or sliced. Drizzle with olive oil.

POTATOES IN THEIR SKINS
with herbed quark

INFO

From being little more than an ornamental plant, the **potato** has since become one of our most important staple foods. In spring and fall you can find new potatoes that can be cooked and eaten with their skins and go wonderfully with salads and herbed quark, as shown here. In some cases, potatoes can be cooked the day before.

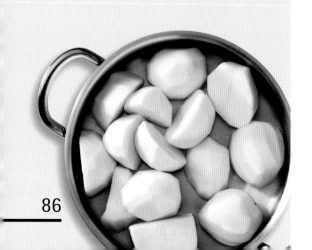

Serves 4

1³/₄ lb (800 g)	*small, waxy new potatoes*
1 lb (500 g)	*quark*
7 tbsp (100 ml)	*yogurt*
3 tbsp	*light cream*
1	*onion*
1	*gherkin*
¹/₂ bunch each	*chives, parsley, dill, chervil and tarragon*
	Salt
	Pepper
25 min.	*preparation time*

Step by step

Scrub the potatoes thoroughly under running water and boil for about 20 minutes. Strain and leave to cool.

Mix together the quark and the yogurt, and stir in the cream.

Peel and chop the onion and finely dice the gherkin. Add to the quark mixture.

Wash the herbs, shake dry, tear the leaves from the stems, and chop.

Fold the herbs into the quark mixture and season with salt and pepper. Add the potatoes and season with salt.

Side dish

To make **meatballs**, combine generous 1 lb (500 g) ground meat with 2 eggs, 1 soaked and squeezed bread roll, 1 chopped onion, salt, pepper, ground paprika, and 2 tablespoons chopped parsley. Shape into balls with moist hands and fry in 2 tablespoons clarified butter for 4 minutes each side.

Side dish

To make **vegetable skewers**, wash, deseed, and dice 1 red bell pepper. Wash and slice 1 zucchini. Wash 4 tomatoes and cut into quarters. Wipe 12 mushrooms with a damp cloth. Alternate the vegetables on skewers and leave to stand for 6 hours in a marinade of 1 tablespoon each chopped parsley, thyme, and rosemary, 2 chopped garlic cloves, 1 cup (250 ml) olive oil, salt, and pepper. Drain well and bake in the oven for 10 minutes.

DIPS
for potatoes in their skins

You simply have to try these three dips, either with potatoes cooked in their skins or with one of our recipe variations.

Chervil cream
Mix 1 bunch chopped chervil with crème fraîche, yogurt, curry powder, ground paprika, and salt. Perfect with potatoes in their skins, au gratin, or goulash.

Wild garlic pesto
Purée wild garlic, parsley, almonds, rapeseed oil, and Parmesan in a blender. Season with salt and pepper. Perfect with potatoes sautéed or wrapped in bacon.

Garlic quark
Mix yogurt, finely diced cucumber, pressed garlic, vinegar, olive oil, salt and pepper. Perfect with potatoes in their skins, au gratin, or sautéed.

Preparation time: 25 minutes

... with eggs and green sauce
Boil $1^3/_4$ lb (800 g) waxy potatoes in their skins for 20 minutes, until cooked. Hard cook 8 eggs. Wash the herbs for the green sauce, chop finely, and mix with soured cream, oil, vinegar, mustard, salt, and pepper. Serve the potatoes with the green sauce and peeled and halved eggs.

Preparation time: 30 minutes

... au gratin
Slice generous 1 lb (500 g) potatoes, season with salt and pepper, and place in a greased gratin dish. Pour over $^1/_2$ cup (120 ml) light cream. Sprinkle with generous $2^1/_2$ cups (300 g) grated Gouda and 3 tablespoons dried breadcrumbs. Bake in a pre-heated oven at 400 °F/200 °C for 15 minutes.

POTATOES IN THEIR SKINS
several variations

Potatoes can be cooked with or without their skins: they can be grated, fried, mashed, used in gratin dishes, served as fries, mixed with flour and used to make gnocchi... the variations are endless. Here's a selection of the quickest!

Preparation time: 25 minutes

... with roast meat, gherkins, and egg

Cut $1^3/_4$ lb (800 g) potatoes into cubes. Dice 2 onions and sweat in 3 tablespoons clarified butter. Fry the potato cubes until crisp. Dice $5^1/_2$ oz (150 g) leftover roast meat and fry with the potatoes. Add 4 beaten eggs and allow to set while stirring. Season with salt and pepper. Serve with gherkins.

Preparation time: 30 minutes

... with bacon and meatloaf

Cut $1^3/_4$ lb (800 g) potatoes into slices. Slice 1 onion into rings. Dice $5^1/_2$ oz (150 g) streaky bacon. Fry in 3 tablespoons clarified butter with the potato and onion slices until crisp. Fry 14 oz (400 g) sliced meatloaf in oil until crispy and add to the potato mixture. Sprinkle with parsley.

Preparation time: 30 minutes

... goulash potatoes

Chop 3 onions and 3 cloves garlic and sweat in 3 tablespoons clarified butter. Add 3 tablespoons paprika and $^1/_4$ teaspoon vinegar. Pour in 1 cup (250 ml) vegetable bouillon and season with salt, pepper, 1 pinch marjoram, and caraway seeds. Cook for 10 minutes. Add 2 cups (500 ml) vegetable bouillon and $2^1/_4$ lb (1 kg) diced potatoes. Brown $5^1/_2$ oz (150 g) sliced pepperoni and stir in. Garnish with light cream and herbs.

Preparation time: 30 minutes

... wrapped in bacon

Boil 12 small, waxy potatoes for 15 minutes. Strain and peel. Brush each potato with butter, wrap in $^1/_2$ slice Gouda and a bacon rasher, and secure with toothpicks. Bake in a pre-heated oven at 350 °F/180 °C for 10 minutes.

MEAT, POULTRY, AND FISH

Schnitzels, steaks, etc. can be fried or grilled in under 15 minutes. Add a quick salad or bread and you have a delicious meal. No junk food in sight, and all prepared in a flash.

Enjoy our colorful collection of meat, poultry, and fish dishes— a great way of adding variety to your cooking, day after day!

BREADED SCHNITZEL
Viennese style

Serves 4

4	cutlets (7 oz/200 g each)
	Salt
	Pepper
2	eggs
2 tbsp	chopped parsley
3 tbsp	all-purpose flour
2 cups (100 g)	dried breadcrumbs
3 tbsp	clarified butter
1	unwaxed lemon, washed and quartered
25 min.	preparation time

INFO

Authentic **Wiener Schnitzel** is a thin slice of veal that is breaded and fried. It is one of Austria's most famous specialties, but has only appeared in cookery books in this form since the end of the 19th century. There is much debate when it comes to traditional side dishes. Potato salad and fried potatoes are both popular and eaten regularly. A less traditional choice, but one which is popular with young people, is French fries.

Step by step

Wash the cutlets, pat dry, and pound between two layers of plastic wrap.

Season the cutlets with salt and pepper.

Whisk the eggs and fold in the parsley. Pour into a shallow dish.

Place the flour and breadcrumbs in two separate dishes.

Coat the cutlets first in flour, then in egg, and finally in breadcrumbs. Shake off any excess breadcrumbs.

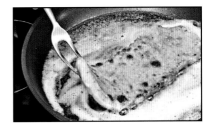

Heat the clarified butter and fry the cutlets for 4 minutes on both sides. Serve with lemon quarters.

Side dish

To make **fried potatoes**, slice 1³/₄ lb (800 g) cooked and cooled potatoes in their skins, fry in 3–4 tablespoons hot oil until golden brown, and season with salt and pepper. Add 1 large chopped onion and diced ham and fry for a few more minutes. Sprinkle with chopped parsley.

SALADS
for schnitzel

Salad goes very well with schnitzel. Choose a green salad of fresh leaves or one that is more hearty and filling.

Tomato and cucumber salad
Cut tomatoes and cucumber into slices. Mix together with a dressing made from vinegar, oil, parsley, and dill.

Potato and bacon salad
Slice waxy potatoes cooked in their skins. Mix with chopped onion, fried, diced bacon, and a dressing made from bouillon, vinegar, oil, salt, and pepper.

Fennel and orange salad
Finely chop or grate 2 fennel. Mix with oranges cut into segments and diced and a dressing of orange juice, lemon juice, oil, salt, and pepper.

BREADED SCHNITZEL
several

Breaded schnitzel tastes just as good warm as it does cold and can be made using veal, pork, or even lamb. As a change from breadcrumbs, try using crispbread, nuts, almonds, coconut flakes, or cheese as a coating. Herbs and spices, e.g. chile, can also be mixed into

Preparation time: 20 minutes

... with a herb coating
Rub $1^{1}/_{4}$ lb (600 g) lamb saddle fillet cut into slices with salt, pepper, and fresh garlic. Put 3 tablespoons flour, 2 beaten eggs, and 4 tablespoons dried breadcrumbs mixed with 3 teaspoons herbes de Provence in 3 separate dishes. Coat the cutlets in flour, egg, and breadcrumbs and fry in clarified butter for 5 minutes on each side.

Preparation time: 20 minutes

... with an almond coating
Pound 4 veal cutlets and season with salt and pepper. Place 3 tablespoons flour, 2 eggs whisked with 3 tablespoons milk, and 5 tablespoons dried breadcrumbs mixed with 3 tablespoons slivered almonds in 3 separate dishes. Coat the cutlets in flour, egg, and the almond mixture. Fry in hot clarified butter for about 5 minutes on each side.

variations

the coating to add extra flavor. Top chefs love to use "mie de pain" as a coating—fresh breadcrumbs made from crustless white bread. Thinly sliced cutlets from the top round of veal are especially delicious when coated with finely grated bread.

Preparation time: 25 minutes

... stuffed with prunes

Cut 4 pork cutlets horizontally. Stuff pockets with 4 oz (120 g) cream cheese and 2 oz (60 g) diced, pitted prunes. Fold the cutlets together and season with salt and pepper. Coat in flour, beaten egg, and crumbled sesame crispbread. Fry in hot clarified butter for about 5 minutes on each side.

Preparation time: 20 minutes

... with a chile coating

Pound 4 turkey cutlets. Brush with a mixture of 4 tablespoons cream cheese, salt, and cayenne. Place 3 tablespoons flour, 2 eggs beaten with 3 tablespoons milk, and 2 cups (100 g) dried breadcrumbs mixed with 2 chopped red chiles and 7 table-spoons (60 g) cornmeal in separate dishes. Coat the cutlets and fry in hot clarified butter for about 3–4 minutes on both sides.

... POULTRY, AND FISH

SIDE DISHES
for schnitzel

Mushrooms and vegetables also make great accompaniments for Viennese-style schnitzel.

Fried cherry tomatoes
Fry cherry tomatoes briefly in the fat used for frying the schnitzel, and season with salt and pepper.

Mixed mushrooms
Stew chanterelles and common-store mushrooms in hot clarified butter with chopped scallions. Add white wine and light cream, and simmer until smooth.

Wilted spinach
Sweat chopped onions. Add washed spinach and allow to wilt. Remove, chop, and season with salt, pepper, and nutmeg. Serve with toasted pine nuts.

95

SCHNITZEL
with ham and sage

Serves 4

4	veal cutlets (4¹/₂ oz/125 g each)
	Salt
	Pepper
4 large	sage leaves
4 slices	air-dried ham
	Toothpicks
2 tbsp	clarified butter
3 tbsp	dry white wine
¹/₂ cup (125 ml)	meat bouillon
20 min.	preparation time

Step by step

Wash, dry, and pound the cutlets. Season with salt and pepper.

Fry the cutlets in hot clarified butter for about 4 minutes on each side. Remove from the pan and keep warm.

Wash the sage leaves and shake them dry.

Add the wine to the pan juices and boil down. Pour in the bouillon and reduce by one third.

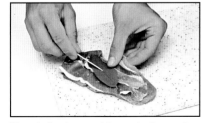

Place 1 slice ham and 1 sage leaf on each cutlet and secure with a wooden toothpick.

Season the sauce with salt and pepper, and serve with the cutlets.

SAGE INFO

With its large, silvery-green leaves and pretty blue flowers, **sage** is a highly decorative plant with an extremely aromatic

flavor. It is particularly recommended for fatty dishes, to aid digestion, and is an essential part of Italian cuisine. For thousands of years, sage has been recognized for its healing powers and is particularly helpful in easing the discomfort caused by respiratory tract infections and sore throats.

CLARIFIED BUTTER INFO

Clarified butter is the only kind of fat made from cow's milk. It is produced by removing the water, milk protein, and lactose from

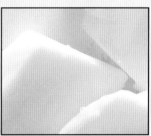

melted butter, leaving behind pure concentrated butter. Clarified butter has a longer shelf life than fresh butter and can be heated to higher temperatures. It is especially good for frying if you're looking for a very tangy flavor. Indian ghee is a form of clarified butter.

SCHNITZEL
several variations

Veal, pork, chicken, and venison cutlets have long been considered classics of the culinary world. The trick is to pound them to make them tender and only fry them for a short while, to prevent them from becoming too dry.

Preparation time: 20 minutes

... with thyme and capers

Marinate 8 pork fillet slices for 30 minutes in a marinade made from 8 tablespoons lemon juice, 1 chopped garlic clove, 4 tablespoons olive oil, and 3 tablespoons fresh thyme leaves. Broil with 1 tablespoon oil for 3 minutes on both sides. Bring the marinade to a boil with 1 cup (250 ml) bouillon. Fold in 3 tablespoons capers. Season with salt and pepper.

Preparation time: 20 minutes

... with Gorgonzola sauce

Pound 4 pork cutlets and season with salt and pepper. Fry in 2 tablespoons clarified butter for about 4 minutes on both sides. Remove and add $1^1/_2$ tablespoons Cognac to the panjuices. Add $^2/_3$ cup (150 ml) light cream and $4^1/_2$ oz (125 g) diced Gorgonzola, and simmer until creamy. Season, then fold in 2 tablespoons chopped chives.

Preparation time: 25 minutes

... with sherry sauce

Pound 4 chicken cutlets and season with salt and pepper. Fry in 2 tablespoons clarified butter for 3 minutes on each side. Add 1 chopped garlic clove. Remove the cutlets and keep warm. Add a generous $^3/_4$ cup (200 ml) meat bouillon and 4 tablespoons sherry to the pan juices. Reduce by a third then add a little more sherry to taste. Serve the sauce with the cutlets.

Preparation time: 30 minutes

... with spicy sauce

Fry 4 turkey cutlets in 2 tablespoons clarified butter for 3 minutes on both sides. Remove and keep warm. Add $1^1/_4$ lb (600 g) canned tomatoes and 3 chopped red chiles to the pan juices and simmer for 20 minutes. Season with $^1/_2$ bunch shredded basil, salt, and cayenne.

SIDE DISHES
for schnitzel

Potatoes in any form go especially well with schnitzel.

Mashed potato

Peel 1³/₄ lb (800 g) mealy potatoes cooked in their skins. Mash with butter and milk, and season with salt, pepper, and nutmeg.

Duchess potatoes

Make mashed potato using 1³/₄ lb (800 g) potatoes cooked in their skins, butter, egg yolk, salt, pepper, and nutmeg. Use a pastry bag to pipe small mounds onto a greased baking sheet. Bake at 425 °F/220 °C for 10 minutes.

Croquette potatoes

Make mashed potato using 1³/₄ lb (800 g) potatoes cooked in their skins. Mix together with flour and eggs. Roll into cylinders, cut into pieces, coat in dried breadcrumbs, and fry in hot fat.

Preparation time: 20 minutes

... with orange sauce

Fry 4 veal cutlets in 2 tablespoons clarified butter for 3 minutes on each side. Keep warm. Sweat 2 chopped shallots in the pan juices. Pour over ¹/₂ cup (125 ml) each bouillon and red wine. Stir in 1 tablespoon chopped thyme and 3 tablespoons each orange juice and orange marmalade, and simmer for 5 minutes. Purée the sauce, and serve with orange slices.

Preparation time: 20 minutes

... with cherry sauce

Marinate 4 venison cutlets in chopped garlic, 2 tablespoons oil, 1 tablespoon soy sauce, 1 teaspoon dried oregano, salt, and pepper for 2 hours. Pat dry. Fry in hot oil for 3 minutes on each side. Remove. Add ¹/₂ cup (125 ml) each red wine and marinade to the juices. Fold in 1 teaspoon mustard powder and 7 oz (200 g) Morello cherries. Thicken with sour cream and flour.

MEATBALLS

with tomato sauce

INFO

Ground meat is muscle meat that has been freshly minced. It is usually pork or beef, but can also be lamb. Ground meat has a higher fat content and is very susceptible to bacteria, so should be cooked immediately. It is mainly used for preparing meatballs, hamburgers, and meat sauces, or as a filling for vegetables, and is combined with herbs and spices to give it an extra kick.

Serves 4

2	onions
1	clove garlic
1/2 bunch	parsley
1³/₄ lb (800 g)	mixed ground meat
1	egg
1	bread roll, soaked and squeezed
	Salt
	Pepper
3 tbsp	oil
14 oz (400 g)	canned tomatoes
	Sugar
2 tbsp	chopped thyme
30 min.	preparation time

100

Step by step

Peel and chop the onions and garlic. Wash the parsley, shake dry, and chop.

Mix together the ground meat, egg, half the chopped onion, garlic, crumbled bread roll, and parsley. Season with salt and pepper.

Shape the meat mixture into balls and fry in 2 tablespoons of oil until crisp and brown on all sides. Keep warm.

Brown the remaining onion in a pan in 1 tablespoon of oil. Add the canned tomatoes and simmer for 15 minutes.

Purée the sauce and season with salt, pepper, sugar, and thyme. Serve the meatballs in the sauce.

Side dish

To make **parsley potatoes**, wash, peel, and halve 1³/₄ lb (800 g) potatoes. Cook in boiling salt water for 15–20 minutes. Strain, leave to steam, and sprinkle with parsley to serve.

Salad

To make **cucumber salad**, peel 1 cucumber and cut into very thin slices. Mix in a bowl with a dressing made from 7 tablespoons (100 ml) light cream, 2 tablespoons white wine vinegar, salt, pepper, sugar to taste, and chopped dill.

SAUCES AND DIPS
for ground meat

Crispy meatballs or ground beef steaks always taste delicious with a hearty sauce or dip.

Ham and caper sauce

Sweat chopped onion, garlic, and diced boiled ham. Add bouillon and wine. Simmer until creamy and stir in capers. Perfect with the fried egg, and sesame crust recipes.

Pepper sauce

Sweat onion, pour over wine, bouillon, and sherry, and boil down. Add light cream and fold in green peppercorns. Season with salt and pepper. Perfect with the fried egg recipe.

Herb dip

Mix together yogurt, sour cream, freshly chopped herbs, salt, and pepper. Perfect with the ewe's milk cheese, and sesame crust recipes.

Preparation time: 30 minutes

... with onion sauce

Mix together $1^3/_4$ lb (800 g) mixed ground meat, 1 soaked and squeezed bread roll, 2 eggs, 2 tablespoons chopped parsley, and 1 chopped onion. Season with salt, pepper, and ground paprika. Shape and fry the meatballs. Sweat 4 onions cut into rings in the juices. Add 1 cup (250 ml) bouillon and reduce by a half. Finish with light cream.

Preparation time: 25 minutes

... with ginger and soy

Combine $1^1/_4$ lb (600 g) mixed ground meat, $^1/_2$ teaspoon grated ginger, $^1/_4$ teaspoon ground coriander, 1 egg, 1 oz (30 g) dried breadcrumbs, 1 tablespoon soy sauce, salt, pepper, and a dash of rice wine. Shape into balls, coat in a mixture of $^2/_3$ cup (100 g) flour, 4 tablespoons cornstarch, 4 tablespoons oil, 7 tablespoons (100 ml) water, and salt. Fry in hot oil.

GROUND MEAT
several variations

These ground meat dishes are quick to prepare. Simply make and fry the meatballs, add a quick sauce, and that's all there is to it! Salad and bread are all you need as accompaniments.

Preparation time: 20 minutes

... filled with ewe's milk cheese

Combine 1³/₄ lb (800 g) ground lamb, 1 soaked and squeezed bread roll, 2 eggs, 2 tablespoons chopped parsley, and 1 chopped onion. Season with salt, pepper, and ground paprika. Shape into meatballs and place a walnut-size piece of ewe's milk cheese in each. Fry in hot oil for 5 minutes on both sides.

Preparation time: 20 minutes

... with a sesame crust

Combine 1³/₄ lb (800 g) mixed ground meat, 2 eggs, 2 cups (100 g) breadcrumbs, 1 chopped onion, 1 finely chopped red chile, salt, and pepper. Shape into balls and coat in 1 cup (125 g) sesame seeds. Fry in hot fat for about 5–10 minutes. Serve with herb baguettes.

Preparation time: 25 minutes

... with onions and bell peppers

Shape 1¹/₄ lb (600 g) mixed ground meat, 1 chopped onion, salt, pepper, and ground paprika into cylinders and fry until crisp. Sauté 2 diced green bell peppers and 1 chopped onion in 1 tablespoon butter. Season with salt, pepper, and chopped oregano, mix with boiled rice, and arrange the meat rolls on top to serve.

Preparation time: 30 minutes

... with fried egg

Combine 1³/₄ lb (800 g) ground beef, 1 chopped onion, 1 egg, 3 tablespoons breadcrumbs mixed with 2 teaspoons chopped nuts, 1 tablespoon mustard, salt, pepper, and ground paprika. Shape into steaks with moist hands and fry in 2 tablespoons clarified butter for 8–10 minutes on each side. Serve each steak with a fried egg.

WOK DISHES
with sweet and sour sauce

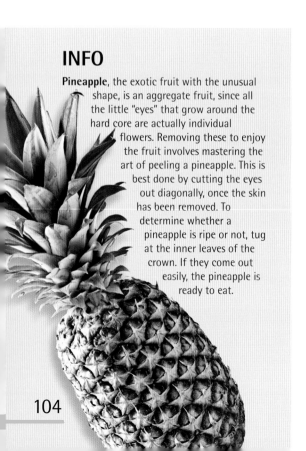

INFO

Pineapple, the exotic fruit with the unusual shape, is an aggregate fruit, since all the little "eyes" that grow around the hard core are actually individual flowers. Removing these to enjoy the fruit involves mastering the art of peeling a pineapple. This is best done by cutting the eyes out diagonally, once the skin has been removed. To determine whether a pineapple is ripe or not, tug at the inner leaves of the crown. If they come out easily, the pineapple is ready to eat.

Serves 4

12 oz (350 g)	*pork cutlet*
3	*cloves garlic*
1	*onion*
2 tbsp	*rapeseed oil*
2 tbsp	*fish sauce*
1 tbsp	*sugar*
	Salt
	Pepper
1	*diced red bell pepper*
1	*diced zucchini*
2	*diced tomatoes*
4 oz (120 g)	*diced pineapple*
	cilantro leaves
25 min.	*preparation time*

Step by step

Wash the meat, pat dry, and cut into thin strips.

Peel the garlic and onion, and chop finely.

Heat the oil in a wok. Brown the garlic, onion, and strips of meat.

Season with the fish sauce, sugar, salt, and pepper. Fry for 4 minutes, stirring continuously.

Add the vegetables, tomatoes, and pineapple. Add water and fry for another 4 minutes. Garnish with cilantro.

Side dish

To make **aromatic rice**, sweat 1 cup (200 g) scented rice (e.g. basmati, jasmine, Texmati) in 1 tablespoon oil. Pour over double the quantity of water, add salt, and stir well. Bring to a boil and simmer for about 15 minutes.

Dip

To make **chile dip**, peel 7 oz (200 g) tomatoes, remove the stalks and seeds, and dice or chop finely. Wash 2 red chiles, deseed, and chop. Peel 1 clove garlic and chop finely. Mix together the tomatoes, chile, garlic, and 1 tablespoon tomato purée, and season with salt and pepper.

WOK DISHES
several variations

The round-bottomed pan used in Chinese cooking can now be found more and more in our part of the world. After all, cooking and frying in a wok is very economical. Dishes can be prepared in an instant and are very healthy, as meat and vegetables are not overcooked.

Preparation time: 20 minutes

... with beef and lemongrass

Marinate 14 oz (400 g) beef strips in egg yolk, cornstarch, and 1 tablespoon soy sauce for 30 minutes. Fry in 2 tablespoons peanut oil and season with salt and pepper. Remove from the pan. Fry chopped onion, garlic, lemongrass, diced red bell pepper, chopped chile, 1 leek cut into strips, and 1 teaspoon grated ginger in the oil for 3 minutes. Add the meat.

Preparation time: 20 minutes

... with omelet, rice noodles, and cilantro

Pour boiling water over 7 oz (200 g) rice noodles and leave to soak. Fry an omelet using 4 beaten eggs, salt, and pepper and cut into strips. Fry 3$^1/_2$ oz (100 g) shrimp in 2 tablespoons oil in a wok for 2 minutes. Remove and fry 2 leeks cut into rings for 2 minutes. Fold in 2 tablespoons each soy sauce and sherry, then add the shrimp, omelet, and glass noodles. Sprinkle with chopped cilantro.

Preparation time: 20 minutes

... with chicken and bamboo shoots

Marinate 12 oz (350 g) chicken cut into strips in 3 tablespoons soy sauce, 1 tablespoon sherry, and 2 tablespoons sesame oil for 30 minutes. Fry in 2 tablespoons hot oil for 2 minutes. Remove. Heat 2 tablespoons oil and fry 2 chopped cloves garlic, 1$^3/_4$ oz (50 g) sugar snap peas, and 4 oz (115 g) bamboo shoots for two minutes. Sprinkle with scallions cut into rings.

Preparation time: 20 minutes

... with sugar snap peas, broccoli, and carrots

Fry 3$^1/_2$ oz (100 g) washed sugar snap peas, 7 oz (200 g) peeled and sliced carrots, and 11 oz (300 g) broccoli florets in 2 tablespoons sesame oil for 4 minutes, stirring continuously. Add 1 clove pressed garlic. Add 2 tablespoons rice wine, 1 tablespoon oyster sauce, 2 tablespoons lemon juice, and 1 tablespoon Worcestershire sauce. Stir in 7 tablespoons (200 ml) water and 1$^1/_2$ teaspoons red curry paste. Simmer for 4 minutes and season.

SIDE DISHES
Wok dishes

These three side dishes can be prepared just as quickly as the wok dishes themselves.

Preparation time: 25 minutes

... with fish, papaya, and chile

Coat 14 oz (400 g) diced pollock in 1 teaspoon five-spice powder and flour. Brown 2 chopped red chiles and 1 chopped onion in 2 tablespoons oil. Add the fish and fry for 1 minute. Fry $3^1/_2$ oz (100 g) each baby corn and diced papaya for 2 minutes. Season with 2 tablespoons soy sauce, 2 tablespoons rice wine, 1 teaspoon sugar, salt, and pepper.

Preparation time: 20 minutes

... with pork, sprouts, and shiitake mushrooms

Fry 9 oz (250 g) pork cut into strips in 1 tablespoon hot oil in a wok. Remove. Fry $4^1/_2$ oz (125 g) shiitake mushrooms and 1 celery stalk cut into slices in a clean wok for 2 minutes. Fold in $3^1/_2$ oz (100 g) bean sprouts and the meat. Add 2 tablespoons oyster sauce and 2 tablespoons tamarind liquid, simmer for 2 minutes, and season with salt and pepper. Sprinkle with 2 tablespoons chopped peanuts.

Rice noodles

Cook rice noodles in freshly boiled salt water according to the pack instructions. Perfect with all recipe variations, excluding omelet with rice noodles.

Fried rice

Fry cooked, drained rice in vegetable oil with beaten eggs and peas. Perfect with all the recipe variations, excluding omelet with rice noodles.

Fried rice noodles

Heat peanut oil in a wok. Fry rice noodles until crispy. Perfect with all the recipe variations, excluding omelet with rice noodles.

CURRY

with beef and bell peppers

	Serves 4
1	*red chile*
2	*shallots*
1 each	*red and green bell pepper*
1¼ lb (600 g)	*stewing beef*
2 tbsp	*peanut oil*
2 tbsp	*red curry paste*
5 oz (140 g)	*canned bamboo shoots, drained*
3	*diced tomatoes*
¾ cup (200 ml)	*coconut milk*
1 tbsp	*light soy sauce*
1 tbsp	*table sugar*
30 min.	*preparation time*

Step by step

Wash the chile and cut in half. Remove the seeds and cut into rings.

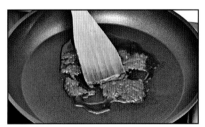

Heat the oil in a pan and brown the curry paste, stirring continuously.

Peel the shallots and cut into rings. Wash and wipe the bell peppers, deseed, and cut into strips.

Add the meat and fry. Add the chile, shallots, bell peppers, bamboo shoots, and tomatoes. Simmer for 3 minutes.

Wash the meat, pat dry, and cut into small cubes.

Pour over the coconut milk and ⅔ cup (150 ml) water. Bring to a boil and cook for about 20 minutes. Season with the soy sauce and sugar.

CHILE PASTE INFO

A good **chile paste** should contain no fewer than 11 different ingredients, ranging from chile pepper, lemongrass, and galangal, through onion and garlic, to

ginger root, coriander, cumin, and pepper. Vegetable ingredients are chopped, cooked in oil, and puréed with spices in a blender. Chile paste can be red or green, depending on the color of the chiles used to make it.

TABLE SUGAR INFO

Table or **granulated sugar** is obtained from sugarcane. Juice is pressed from the plant and combined with lime to bind impurities. This is then clarified and, with further heating, sugar crystals and molasses are deposited. These crystals are

separated from the molasses as a result of refinement with water, with all minerals passing to the molasses. The more frequently the process is repeated, the whiter the sugar becomes.

SIDE DISHES
for curry

Rice is, and always will be, the best side dish for curry, and can be prepared in countless different ways.

Herb rice
Cook $1\frac{1}{4}$ cups (250 g) basmati rice according to pack instructions. Toss in hot butter and chopped herbs.

Lemon rice
Cook $1\frac{1}{4}$ cups (250 g) rice according to pack instructions. Fold in chopped cashews and lemon juice.

Coconut rice
Cook $1\frac{1}{4}$ cups (250 g) rice according to pack instructions, in double the quantity of coconut milk. Season with salt and jaggery (palm sugar).

CURRY
several

Curry powder is a blend of a number of different spices that can be bought ready to use. On its own, the word "curry" is understood by its creators to mean a dish containing sauce. In India, chefs concoct their own recipes for blends of spices, also known as

Preparation time: 30 minutes

... with pork, bamboo shoots, and tomatoes
Season $1\frac{1}{4}$ lb (600 g) pork cutlet cut into strips and fry in 2 tablespoons oil. Remove. Sweat 1 onion cut into rings. Add 4 diced tomatoes, 1 tablespoon grated ginger, and 1 teaspoon turmeric powder, the meat, $4\frac{1}{2}$ oz (125 g) drained, canned bamboo shoots, and $\frac{1}{2}$ cup (125 ml) bouillon. Season with salt and sugar and simmer for 15 minutes.

Preparation time: 25 minutes

... with fish and potatoes
Rub $1\frac{1}{4}$ lb (600 g) diced fish fillet with salt and 2 teaspoons turmeric. Fry in 2 tablespoons oil for 2 minutes. Remove. Fry 2 peeled and diced potatoes in the pan juices for 3 minutes. Add 1 teaspoon cumin, 1 teaspoon ground coriander, and 1 finely chopped green chile. Pour over $1\frac{1}{4}$ cups (300 ml) bouillon and simmer for 10 minutes. Fold in the fish and season with salt and pepper.

variations

garam masala, which they are often reluctant to divulge to others. The following four recipe variations will give you an idea of the infinite variety of curry dishes.

In India, curry is also served with yogurt, vegetables, and lentils (dhal). Give it a go!

Preparation time: 30 minutes

... with chicken, apple, and mint

Flour generous 1 lb (500 g) chicken breast fillet, cut into strips, and season with salt and pepper. Brown in 2 tablespoons oil and remove. Sweat chopped onion and 1 diced apple, sprinkle with 2 teaspoons curry powder, and pour over 7 tablespoons (100 ml) each apple juice and chicken bouillon. Stir in 3 tablespoons light cream. Add the meat and sprinkle with chopped mint.

Raita (cucumber yogurt)

Mix together yogurt, deseeded and diced cucumber, chopped shallot, garlic, cumin, chopped parsley, salt, and pepper.

Preparation time: 30 minutes

... with lamb, apricots, and peanuts

Sweat 1 chopped onion, 1 teaspoon grated ginger, and 1 crushed garlic clove in oil. Add $^1/_2$ teaspoon each cumin and cardamom, 2 teaspoons tomato purée, and $1^1/_4$ lb (600 g) lamb fillet, cut into strips. Brown the meat, then add $^1/_2$ teaspoon garam masala and pour over $^2/_3$ cup (150 ml) coconut milk. Simmer for 15 minutes. Add chopped apricots and peanuts and cook for a further 3 minutes.

Sautéed cucumbers

Sauté peeled and deseeded cucumbers in sesame and chile oil. Season with salt, soy sauce, sugar, and dill.

Lentil purée (dhal)

Sweat chopped chile, garlic, onion, and curry powder, then add tomatoes with grated ginger and turmeric. Stir in cooked lentils and sour cream. Season with salt.

PAN-FRIED FISH
with mixed vegetables

INFO

Lemon sole belongs to the flounder family. It can be found in the northeastern Atlantic Ocean and grows up to 24 in. (60 cm) long. Lemon sole is firm, white, and has few bones. Apart from-pan frying, it is particularly good for grilling, broiling, or poaching. Alternatively, cut fillets into cubes and add to curries, or dip in batter and deep fry.

Serves 4

9 oz (250 g)	*cauliflower*
9 oz (250 g)	*broccoli*
1	*fennel*
3 tbsp	*olive oil*
1³/₄ oz (50 g)	*pitted black olives*
2 tbsp	*lemon juice*
²/₃ cup (150 ml)	*white wine*
3 tbsp	*butter*
	Salt
	Pepper
1³/₄ lb (800 g)	*lemon sole fillet, cut into large pieces*
30 min.	*preparation time*

Step by step

Wash the cauliflower and broccoli. Cut into florets.

Wash the fennel and remove any hard leaves. Cut the fennel into strips.

Heat 2 tablespoons of oil and sweat the vegetables, stirring continuously. Stir in the olives.

Add the lemon juice and white wine. Stir in the butter. Season.

Wash the fish, pat dry, and fry in the remaining oil for 2 minutes on both sides. Carefully mix with the vegetables.

Side dish

To make **herb pasta**, boil 14 oz (400 g) spaghetti in salt water until al dente. While cooking, chop $\frac{1}{2}$ bunch each basil, dill, parsley, and chives. Sweat 1 chopped garlic clove in 2 tablespoons oil. Add the herbs and toss. Add the drained pasta and heat briefly.

Side dish

To make **braised mushrooms**, clean 9 oz (250 g) mixed mushrooms (e.g. common-store mushrooms, chanterelles, oyster mushrooms) with a damp cloth and, if necessary, cut into small pieces. Peel and chop 1 onion. Sauté the onion in 1 tablespoon hot oil. Add the mushrooms and fry for 5 minutes, stirring continuously. Add 3 tablespoons sherry and 7 tablespoons (100 ml) bouillon. Boil down, season with salt and pepper, and sprinkle with chopped parsley.

SIDE DISHES
for pan-fried fish

Complement the delicate flavor of pan-fried fish with toasted bread, potatoes, or rice.

Garlic baguette

Cut baguettes in half lengthwise, spread with garlic butter (mix together butter and crushed garlic), and warm in the broiler. Perfect with all recipe variations.

Buttered potatoes

Cook 1¼ lb (600 g) small potatoes in their skins. Peel and toss in hot butter. Perfect with pan-fried fish with ratatouille, and spinach.

Tomato rice

Cook 1¼ cups (250 g) rice according to the pack instructions. While cooking, stir in 3 tablespoons ready-made tomato pesto. Perfect with pan-fried fish with seafood, and Parma ham.

Preparation time: 20 minutes

... with Parma ham and carrots

Season 4 wolf fish fillets with salt and cayenne, and wrap each in 1 slice Parma ham. Fry in 1 tablespoon clarified butter for 2 minutes on both sides. Keep warm. Sweat 14 oz (400 g) young carrots sliced diagonally in 2 tablespoons oil. Add 2 pressed garlic cloves then stir in lemon juice and 2 tablespoons Marsala.

Preparation time: 20 minutes

... with spinach and chickpeas

Coat 1¾ lb (800 g) salmon fillet in flour and 1 teaspoon ground paprika. Fry in 1 tablespoon oil for about 1 minute on each side, remove, and keep warm. Cut the white parts of ½ bunch scallions into rings, sweat in 1 tablespoon oil, and add 9 oz (250 g) spinach cut into strips. Cook for 2 minutes. Stir in 9 oz (250 g) chickpeas. Season, and serve the salmon with the vegetables.

PAN-FRIED FISH
several variations

Fish is quick to prepare and very healthy. Serve with vegetables for an easy-to-digest and low-calorie meal. The following recipe variations show different ways of preparing fish and seafood.

Preparation time: 20 minutes

... with olives, broccoli, and cherry tomatoes

Season 1³/₄ lb (800 g) pike-perch fillet with herb salt and cayenne. Coat in flour and fry in 1 tablespoon oil for about 2 minutes. Sweat 7 oz (200 g) blanched broccoli florets and 1³/₄ oz (50 g) chopped, pitted olives in 1 tablespoon butter. Add 7 oz (200 g) cherry tomatoes and simmer for 2 minutes. Add the juice of 1 orange. Stir in toasted pine nuts.

Preparation time: 30 minutes

... with celery, pineapple, and sprouts

Sweat 1 celery stalk cut into pieces in 1 tablespoon oil. Add 2 tablespoons oyster sauce, 2 tablespoons soy sauce, and 3 tablespoons pineapple juice. Stir in 3¹/₂ oz (100 g) mixed sprouts and 7 oz (200 g) pineapple cubes. Coat 1³/₄ lb (800 g) pieces of cod fillet in a batter of scant 1 cup (125 g) all-purpose flour, ¹/₂ cup (125 ml) beer, salt, and the beaten white of 1 egg. Fry in hot oil. Drain and fold into the vegetables.

Preparation time: 25 minutes

... with ratatouille vegetables

Dice 7 oz (200 g) eggplant and fry with 7 oz (200 g) diced zucchini for 3 minutes. Add 2 peeled, diced beefsteak tomatoes and season with salt, pepper, chopped thyme, and rosemary. Simmer for 10 minutes. Cut 1³/₄ lb (800 g) pollock fillet into pieces, coat in seasoned flour, fry in 2 tablespoons oil, and serve on the vegetables.

Preparation time: 20 minutes

... with seafood

Sweat 1 diced red bell pepper, 1 onion cut into rings, and 1 diced celery stalk in 2 tablespoons oil. Add 1³/₄ lb (750 g) frozen seafood (thawed) and 5¹/₂ oz (150 g) shelled shrimp, and fry for 5 minutes. Stir in 1 chopped garlic clove and 1 teaspoon each saffron and ground paprika. Season with salt and pepper, and sprinkle with chopped parsley.

ROSEMARY INFO

Rosemary is a typically Mediterranean shrub that imparts a highly aromatic flavor, thanks to its essential oil. When in bloom, it produces pretty blue flowers. Its

leaves are like needles attached to stems, which can also be used to make grilled skewers. Rosemary forms part of a mixture of herbs we call "herbes de Provence," and gives potatoes, Mediterranean vegetables, meat, fish, and poultry a unique taste. Chopped finely or crushed, it can be used when braising, frying, and grilling.

PARSLEY INFO

Parsley is probably the best known and most popular herb used in cooking besides chives. The two main types are curly and flat-leaf, or Italian parsley, the latter being more aromatic. Parsley can be used to season salads and soups, sauces and

dips, quark, and butter, as well as vegetables, meat, and fish. Parsley salad is particularly tasty. Parsley should always be added just before serving, as it loses vitamins during cooking.

Serves 4

4	*turkey breast fillets*
	Salt
	Pepper
	Flour
1¹/₂ tbsp (20 g)	*butter*
1 sprig	*rosemary*
¹/₂ bunch	*flat-leaf parsley*
8	*cherry tomatoes*
25 min.	*preparation time*

Step by step

Remove the skin and tendons from the turkey fillets, wash, and pat dry.

Tear rosemary and parsley leaves from their stalks and chop finely.

Season the meat with salt and pepper and dust with flour.

Coat the fried turkey breast fillets in the herbs.

Heat the butter in a pan and fry the turkey fillets for about 3 minutes on both sides.

Bake with the tomatoes in a preheated oven at 400 °F/200 °C for 8 minutes.

POULTRY
with herbs and cherry tomatoes

SIDE DISHES
for poultry

Mashed or fried potatoes are the perfect accompaniment for tasty fried poultry.

Mashed sweet potato
Cook 1¹/₄ lb (600 g) peeled sweet potatoes and mash with grated ginger, salt and pepper. Fold in butter. Perfect with duck breast.

Spicy potatoes
Sweat 1¹/₄ lb (600 g) sliced potatoes with fennel seeds, chile powder, oil, garlic, and tomato purée in a pan. Add a little bouillon and simmer for 15 minutes. Perfect with chicken and turkey.

Fried potatoes
Peel potatoes, cut into slices, and sauté in a pan in hot clarified butter until crispy. Perfect with all recipe variations.

POULTRY
several

Poultry meat is especially popular with calorie counters and children. Those watching their weight like it due to its low fat content, while it is a favorite with children because of its delicate flavor. The following recipes use only lean chicken breast meat. Another advantage of poultry is that it can be prepared

Preparation time: 15 minutes

... with capers and lemons
Pound 4 chicken cutlets, season with salt and pepper, and coat in flour. Fry in 2 tablespoons hot oil for about 3 minutes on each side. Keep warm. Heat 5 tablespoons butter in a pan. Add 2 tablespoons drained capers, 2 segmented and sliced organic lemons, and ¹/₂ bunch chopped parsley and simmer briefly.

Preparation time: 20 minutes

... au gratin, with ham
Pound 4 turkey breast fillets and season with salt and pepper. Fry in 2 tablespoons hot clarified butter for about 4 minutes on each side. Remove and drain. Top each fillet with 1 slice each boiled ham and Gouda, place in an ovenproof dish, and bake at 400 °F/200 °C for 10 minutes.

SIDE DISHES
for poultry

Besides potatoes, vegetables and salad make great side dishes for fried poultry.

Sweet corn and leek
Sweat leeks cut into rings in butter. Stir in canned, drained sweet corn. Add herbes de Provence and crème fraîche. Perfect with chicken.

Baked pumpkin
Cut pumpkin into slices and deseed. Brush with seasoning oil (salt and cayenne) and bake at 350 °F/180 °C for 20 minutes. Perfect with all recipe variations.

Mango pasta
Mix 7 oz (200 g) cooked pasta with $1/2$ mango cut into strips. Pour over a dressing made from salad cream, the remaining mango (puréed), lemon juice, salt, and pepper. Perfect with chicken and turkey.

variations

quickly; it must, however, always be cooked very thoroughly due to the risk of salmonella infection, which can be particularly dangerous for children, pregnant women, and elderly people. Poultry is cooked when its juices run clear, not pink.

Preparation time: 30 minutes

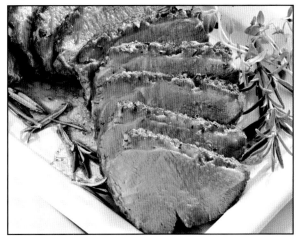

... with a herb and mustard crust
Remove the skin from $1^1/_4$ lb (600 g) duck breast and fry in 2 tablespoons hot oil for about 5 minutes on each side. Mix 3 tablespoons mustard, 1 teaspoon dried thyme, rosemary, tarragon, salt, and pepper, and rub over the duck breast. Cover and fry for a further 10 minutes. Cut into slices.

Preparation time: 20 minutes

... with vegetable salad
Season 4 chicken breast fillets with salt and pepper and fry in 1 tablespoon clarified butter for 2 minutes on each side. Place in an ovenproof dish and bake at 350 °F/180 °C for 15 minutes. Cut 7 oz (200 g) each carrots and zucchini into strips and fry in 1 tablespoon oil for 2 minutes. Mix with a dressing of 1 teaspoon honey, 3 tablespoons orange juice, 2 tablespoons lemon juice, 2 tablespoons oil, salt, and pepper.

POACHED FISH
with mustard and cream sauce

INFO

Salmon travel long distances from salt water to fresh water in order to spawn, and are able to adapt to varying concentrations of salt. Nowadays, salmon is one of the most popular fish used in cooking. Ranging from orangey pink to dark red in color, it is rich in heart-protective omega-3 fatty acids. It can be eaten raw, cooked, fried, and smoked. When buying wild salmon, look out for the sustainable fishing symbol.

Serves 4

4	salmon steaks
3 tbsp	lemon juice
	Salt and pepper
2 cups (500 ml)	fish bouillon
1	onion, peeled and chopped
1	carrot, peeled and cut into strips
1	bay leaf
1/2 cup (125 ml)	dry white wine
2	shallots
2 tbsp	clarified butter
1/2 cup (125 g)	crème fraîche
3 tbsp	mustard
	Sugar
3 tbsp	finely chopped parsley
25 min.	preparation time

Step by step

Drizzle the salmon steaks with 2 table-spoons of lemon juice. Season with salt and pepper.

Bring the fish bouillon, vegetables, bay leaf, remaining lemon juice, and wine to a boil, and poach the salmon in this stock for 8 minutes.

Peel and chop the shallots. Sweat in hot clarified butter until soft.

Add 4 tablespoons of the stock and the crème fraîche, and reduce. Stir in the mustard and 3 more tablespoons of stock, and season with salt, pepper, and sugar.

Serve the salmon steaks with the cream and mustard sauce. Sprinkle with chopped parsley.

Side dish

Rice with spinach and peas: cook 2 cups (400 g) long-grain rice in salt water for 15 minutes. Sweat 7 oz (200 g) each chopped spinach and frozen peas in 2 tablespoons peanut oil. Add 7 tablespoons (100 ml) vegetable bouillon and 3 tablespoons soy sauce. Season with salt, pepper, and nutmeg. Strain the rice and stir into the vegetable mixture.

Side dish

Bunched carrots: remove the tops from 1–2 bunches carrots, scrape thoroughly under running water, and cook in boiling salt water for about 7 minutes, so they remain firm. Drain. Toss briefly in a pan in 1 tablespoon butter.

121

FISH DISHES
several variations

Poached fish is very easy to digest and is ready to serve in minutes. Experiment with fillets, steaks, and whole fish.

Preparation time: 25 minutes

... with an Asian marinade on vegetables

Make a marinade with 3 teaspoons honey, 5 tablespoons olive oil, 3 tablespoons lemon juice, and 3 tablespoons teriyaki sauce, and soak 4 pollock fillets for 10 minutes. Cut 1 red and 1 green bell pepper into strips, drizzle with 2 tablespoons oil, and roast for 10 minutes at 425 °F/220 °C. Place the marinated fish on top and return to the oven for 10 minutes. Season with salt and pepper.

Preparation time: 25 minutes

... with vegetable vinaigrette

Drizzle 8 salmon trout fillets with lemon juice and season with salt and pepper. Simmer in 2 cups (500 ml) fish bouillon and wine for 6–7 minutes. Sweat 1 celery stalk, 1 zucchini, 1 red bell pepper, and 2 carrots (all diced) in 3 tablespoons oil in a pan with garlic and 4 slices lemon, for 5 minutes. Mix with 3 tablespoons lemon juice, sugar, 5 tablespoons oil, salt, and pepper.

Preparation time: 20 minutes

... with pistachio and Parmesan cream

Season 1³/₄ lb (800 g) cod fillet with salt and pepper. Sprinkle with lemon juice. Cook for 6 minutes in a stock made from 1 cup (250 ml) white wine, diced casserole vegetables, and 4 tablespoons butter. Mix 1 bunch each finely chopped dill, parsley, and chives with 3 tablespoons ground pistachios, ¹/₄ cup (30 g) grated Parmesan, 5 tablespoons olive oil, and 6 tablespoons stock. Season with salt and pepper.

Preparation time: 20 minutes

... with cucumber

Sweat 2 peeled, deseeded cucumbers cut into rings in 1 tablespoon oil. Dust with 2 teaspoons flour. Add 10 tablespoons (150 g) crème fraîche and generous ³/₄ cup (200 ml) fish bouillon and stir in 2 tablespoons mild mustard. Simmer for 10 minutes. Add 1¹/₂ lb (700 g) pike perch fillet, cut into cubes, and cook for 5 minutes. Add seasoning. Sprinkle with 2 tablespoons chopped dill.

SAUCES
for fish

Poached fish goes perfectly with sauces. Those shown below are bound to keep fish and sauce lovers equally happy.

Preparation time: 20 minutes

... with wine cream

Beat 7 tablespoons (100 ml) dry white wine with 3 egg yolks in a bain marie until fluffy. After 10 minutes, stir in 7 tablespoons (100 g) cold butter cut into small pieces. Season with salt, pepper, and lemon juice. Season 4 wolf fish fillets with salt and pepper and poach in 2 cups (500 ml) wine and vegetable stock for 7 minutes. Serve with the wine cream.

Preparation time: 20 minutes

... with herbs and béchamel sauce

Make a roux with 3 tablespoons butter and flour. Add 1 cup (250 ml) bouillon and generous $3/4$ cup (200 ml) light cream and cook until creamy, stirring continuously. Stir in 1 bunch chopped flat-leaf parsley, $1/2$ bunch each chopped chives and chervil. Add seasoning. Purée in a blender. Drizzle $1 1/4$ lb (600 g) salmon fillet with lemon juice, cut into strips, and simmer in the sauce for 3 minutes.

Orange and cream sauce

Sweat chopped shallots in butter. Add cream, wine, and fish bouillon. Reduce by half. Stir in orange juice and segmented, diced orange. Perfect with all white fish.

Mushroom sauce

Sweat chopped scallions and mushrooms in oil. Add crème fraîche and fish bouillon. Season with salt and pepper, and beat in an egg yolk. Perfect with all white fish.

Aniseed sauce

Make a roux using milk and add fish bouillon. Stir in egg yolk with pastis (anise-based aperitif) and use to thicken the sauce. Stir in small pieces of cold butter. Perfect with salmon.

BEEF STROGANOFF

with mushrooms and beet

Serves 4

1¹/₄ lb (600 g)	*beef fillet*
7 oz (200 g)	*mushrooms*
2	*shallots*
5¹/₂ oz (150 g)	*gherkins*
5¹/₂ oz (150 g)	*beet (pre-cooked)*
2 tbsp	*oil*
	Salt
	Pepper
¹/₂ cup (125 ml)	*beef bouillon*
10 tbsp (150 g)	*sour cream*
1 tbsp	*mustard*
25 min.	*preparation time*

BEEF STROGANOFF INFO

Beef stroganoff, prepared using the finest beef, is attributed to the wealthy Russian Stroganow family, said to have created the dish in the 19th century for a cooking competition in St. Petersburg. Variations on the traditional recipe include adding vinegar, lemon juice, or mustard for a slightly more acidic taste. True food connoisseurs like to finish it off with a splash of Cognac.

Step by step

Wash the meat, pat dry, and cut into strips. Wipe the mushrooms, and cut into small pieces.

Sweat the mushrooms in the pan juices and add to the meat. Heat the rest of the oil and sweat the shallots until soft.

Peel the shallots and chop finely. Cut the gherkins and beet into strips.

Pour over the bouillon and reduce a little. Stir in the sour cream and mustard. Season with salt and pepper.

Heat 1 tablespoon of oil in a pan and brown the strips of meat. Season and remove.

Return the mushrooms and meat to the pan. Stir in the gherkins and beet. Heat briefly.

BEET INFO

Beet is a red tuber, also known as red beet and garden beet. Its most distinctive feature is its intense, red color, derived from the pigment betanin, which is also used for coloring jelly and candy. Beet should be cooked along with its skin, otherwise the color will bleed and all its nutrients be transferred into the water. It can, however, also be served raw. Red beets are an essential ingredient

in many traditional dishes such as borscht, Labskaus, and beef stroganoff, giving them their distinctive flavor.

SIDE DISHES
for sliced meat

Combine sliced meat with a hearty side dish such as rösti, polenta, or mash.

Swiss rösti
Peel and grate $1^3/_4$ lb (800 g) potatoes. Shape into patties. Fry in hot clarified butter on both sides until crispy. Perfect with "Zürcher Geschnetzelte" (sliced meat, Zurich-style).

Polenta
Sweat $1^3/_4$ cups (250 g) cornmeal in oil. Add double the quantity of water and simmer gently until the liquid is absorbed. Season with salt, pepper, and chopped parsley. Perfect with the duck recipe.

Potato and celery mash
Mash 14 oz (400 g) boiled potatoes and 7 oz (200 g) braised celery. Fold in butter and light cream. Season with salt, pepper, and nutmeg. Perfect with the liver and sausage variations.

MEAT STRIPS
several

Small strips of meat of any kind are quick to prepare and taste fabulous when served with vegetables, mushrooms, and creamy or spicy sauces. Besides beef stroganoff, one famous dish is "Zürcher Geschnetzelte," a Swiss dish that is traditionally made with

Preparation time: 20 minutes

... with liver and apples
Brown $1^3/_4$ lb (600 g) calf's liver cut into strips in 2 tablespoons clarified butter for 2 minutes. Season with salt and remove. Sweat 7 oz (200 g) chopped red onions in the pan juices and add 2 diced apples. Add generous $3/_4$ cup (200 ml) each bouillon and light cream. Simmer for 2 minutes and stir in the liver. Thicken with cornstarch and season with salt, pepper, and sage.

Preparation time: 20 minutes

... with spicy sausage and cheese
Fry 11 oz (300 g) each bologna and salami, cut into strips, in 2 tablespoons oil. Remove. Sweat 2 onions in the pan juices. Add 7 tablespoons (100 ml) bouillon and $1^1/_4$ cups (300 ml) milk, and reduce by a third. Stir in 1 teaspoon mustard and 1 tablespoon cream cheese with herbs. Fold in the sausage meat and 2 scallions cut into rings. Season with salt and pepper, and sprinkle with chopped parsley.

SIDE DISHES
for meat strips

Rice or homemade egg noodles are always a good choice to serve with sliced meat dishes.

Saffron rice
Cook 1¹/₄ cups (250 g) white rice in double the quantity of salt water, with ground saffron.

Wild rice
Cook 1 cup (200 g) wild rice in 2¹/₂ cups (600 ml) salt water. Drain well, and toss in hot butter before serving.

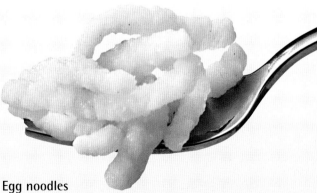

Egg noodles
Prepare a dough using 3 scant cups (400 g) all-purpose flour, 4 eggs, water, and salt. Pass through a pasta machine into boiling water. Cook for 3 minutes. Perfect with "Zürcher Geschnetzelte," and with the liver, and sausage recipe variations.

variations

veal and calf's kidneys. Plenty of other dishes can be prepared using strips of meat. Here are four recipe variations that taste great and are ready to eat in a matter of minutes!

Preparation time: 20 minutes

... with duck and bell peppers
Season 1³/₄ lb (800 g) duck breast, cut into strips, with salt and pepper. Fry for 3 minutes in 2 tablespoons oil. Sweat 1 red and 1 green bell pepper, cut into strips, 1 each chopped chile and garlic clove in the pan juices. Bring to a boil with 4 tablespoons each soy sauce and water. Add the meat and 2 scallions cut into rings. Season with salt and pepper.

Preparation time: 20 minutes

... with veal and mushrooms
Thinly slice 1³/₄ lb (750 g) veal cutlet. Season with salt and pepper, and brown in 2 tablespoons clarified butter for 3 minutes. Remove. Sweat 3¹/₂ oz (100 g) mushrooms and 2 chopped shallots in the pan juices. Dust with flour and add 7 tablespoons (100 ml) white wine and bouillon. Reduce by a half, add 1²/₃ cups (400 ml) light cream, fold in the meat, and season with salt, pepper, nutmeg, and lemon.

MINUTE SIRLOINS
with herb butter

INFO

Cooking **steak** properly requires a little intuition and experience. Some people like it rare, some medium and light pink, while others like it well done. You should use a fat that can be heated to high temperatures, such as corn oil or clarified butter. This is to prevent the meat from drying out if it needs to be fried for a while. Let the fat get really hot before adding the steaks, so that their surfaces are sealed straightaway and the juices retained inside.

Serves 4

¹/₂ bunch	*mixed herbs*
3¹/₂ tbsp (50 g)	*butter*
	Salt
	Pepper
1 tsp	*lemon juice*
4	*minute sirloins (6 oz/175 g each)*
3 tbsp	*clarified butter*
30 min.	*preparation time*

Step by step

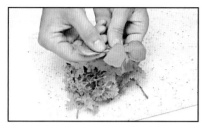

Wash the herbs, shake dry, and tear the leaves from the stalks. Chop finely.

Mix the herbs with the softened butter, salt, pepper, and lemon. Wrap in aluminum foil and place in the freezer to set.

Wash the steaks, pat dry, and pound lightly.

Heat the clarified butter and fry the steaks for between 2 and 8 minutes each side, according to taste.

After frying, season the steaks with salt and pepper. Serve each steak with 1–2 slices of herb butter.

Side dish

To make **French fries**, peel 1¼ lb (600 g) waxy potatoes, cut into matchstick shapes, rinse under hot water, and pat dry. Heat 4 cups (1 liter) fat and fry the potatoes for 7 minutes. Remove, leave to cool, and then fry for a further 3-4 minutes until crispy on the outside.

Salad

To make **mixed salad**, wash and slice ½ bunch radishes and peel and slice ½ cucumber. Cut each of 4 tomatoes into 8 wedges. Tear 1 head of oak leaf lettuce into small pieces and mix all the ingredients together. Make a dressing from 3 tablespoons white wine vinegar, 1 teaspoon tarragon vinegar, 4 table-spoons olive oil, 1 teaspoon soy sauce, salt, pepper, chopped parsley, and chives. Pour over the salad.

129

SAUCES AND DIPS
for steak

Serve fried steak with a spicy sauce or dip for a perfect taste sensation.

Curry sauce
Purée soaked dried apricots and mix with mayonnaise, crème fraîche, curry powder, salt, pepper, and sugar. Perfect with pork and veal steaks.

Gorgonzola dip
Combine Gorgonzola, butter, and yogurt. Fold in chopped chives. Perfect with lamb and beef steaks.

Hot chile sauce
Mix together vinegar, lemon juice, chopped onions, garlic, chiles, radishes, olive oil, salt, and pepper. Perfect with beef and lamb steaks.

Preparation time: 20 minutes

... with red wine and peppercorn sauce
Score the fat of 4 top round steaks and fry in 3 tablespoons clarified butter for about 4–6 minutes on each side. Season with salt and pepper. Sweat 1 chopped red onion and $^1/_2$ chopped red chile in the pan juices. Pour over $1^1/_4$ cups (300 ml) red wine and reduce by a third. Fold in 1 tablespoon green peppercorns and thicken slightly.

Preparation time: 15 minutes

... with olive and anchovy butter
Mix together 5 tablespoons softened butter, salt, pepper, 1 teaspoon grated lemon rind, 10 pitted and chopped black olives, 2 chopped anchovies, and 1 finely chopped shallot. Leave to set in the freezer. Season 4 pork loin steaks with salt and pepper and fry in 2 tablespoons hot clarified butter for 3–4 minutes on each side. Serve with the herb butter.

MINUTE SIRLOINS
several variations

A meal of lean steak and crispy salad is not just for athletes. The healthy combination of protein, vitamins, and minerals is good for everyone, and tastes delicious. Try adding a tasty sauce—and don't forget a fresh baguette, to soak up the last drops!

Preparation time: 15 minutes

... with dried fruit

Fry 4 veal steaks in 2 tablespoons oil for 2–3 minutes on each side. Season with salt and pepper, and keep warm. Sweat 2 chopped onions with 1 teaspoon sugar in the pan juices. Pour over 4 tablespoons chopped dried fruit, 1 tablespoon balsamic vinegar, and $^1/_2$ cup (120 ml) white wine. Simmer for 4 minutes. Season with salt and pepper.

Preparation time: 15 minutes

... with cherry tomatoes and arugula

Mix together 2 tablespoons olive oil, 2 teaspoons chopped rosemary, chopped garlic, salt, and pepper. Brush 4 lamb loin steaks and marinate for 20 minutes. Fry in 1 tablespoon oil for 3 minutes on each side. Remove, cut into slices, and arrange on 1 bunch arugula dressed with vinegar. Toss 7 oz (200 g) cherry tomatoes in the pan juices and serve with the meat.

Preparation time: 20-25 minutes

... with mushrooms and onion

Fry 4 x 1 lb (450-g) T-bone steaks in 2 tablespoons clarified butter for 3–8 minutes each side, according to taste. Remove from the pan, season, and leave to stand. Sweat 11 oz (300 g) chanterelles and 7 oz (200 g) onion, cut into rings, in the juices. Add 2 tablespoons Cognac. Season with salt and pepper and sprinkle with parsley.

Preparation time: 20 minutes

... with a cheese and herb crust

Use a blender to purée $^1/_2$ bunch parsley, 2 sprigs thyme, 5 sage leaves, 1 oz (30 g) white bread, and 3 tablespoons (20 g) Parmesan. Mix with salt and pepper. Fry 4 slices beef fillet in 2 tablespoons hot clarified butter for 2–3 minutes each side. Remove from the pan, place on aluminum foil, and brush with the herb and cheese mixture. Broil for 2–3 minutes.

131

DESSERTS

Sweet dishes are the perfect way to round off a quick meal. Here, we've opted for light and airy mousse, crispy waffles, fresh fruit salads, and desserts made with quark.

Some can be served on their own as sweet main dishes. Alternatively, surprise visitors with a quick and easy flan topped with fruit, cream, or marzipan to go with their coffee.

WAFFLES

with cinnamon and sugar

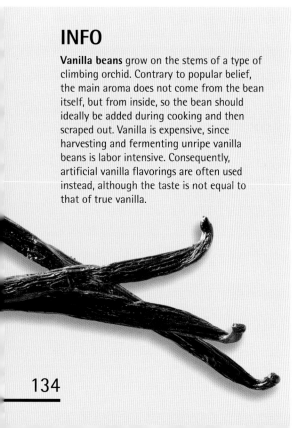

Serves 4

8¹/₂ tbsp (125 g)	butter
5 tbsp	sugar
3 tbsp	vanilla sugar
	Salt
3	eggs, separated
1³/₄ cups (250 g)	all-purpose flour
¹/₂ tsp	baking powder
1 cup (250 ml)	milk
1 cup (250 ml)	mineral water
	Fat for the waffle iron
	Cinnamon and sugar to sprinkle on top
30 min.	preparation time

Step by step

Beat the butter, sugar, vanilla sugar, and 1 pinch salt in a bowl, until fluffy.

Separate the eggs and fold the egg yolks into the mixture.

Mix together the flour and baking powder, and gradually stir into the mixture with the milk and mineral water.

Fold in the stiffly beaten egg whites.

Cook 8 waffles in a greased waffle iron. Sprinkle with cinnamon and sugar.

Sauce

Vanilla sauce: scrape out 1 vanilla bean. Boil the bean, seeds, generous $^3/_4$ cup (200 ml) light cream, and 1 cup (250 ml) milk. Simmer for 10 minutes, then remove the vanilla bean. Mix together 1 tablespoon sugar, 4 egg yolks, and 1 teaspoon cornstarch. Stir into the hot, but not boiling, sauce.

Side dish

Strawberries with mint: sort, wash, and pat dry generous 1lb (500 g) strawberries. Cut into small pieces and mix in a bowl with 1 tablespoon sugar. Sprinkle with 2 tablespoons mint liqueur. Serve with mint leaves and waffles.

WAFFLES
several variations

Waffles are popular with adults and kids alike. Enjoy as a dessert, with coffee in the afternoon, or as a snack in between meals. Waffle batter is quick to prepare, and the toppings are virtually endless. Choose between fruit, sauces, ice cream, and lots more.

Preparation time: 30 minutes

... with hot cherries
Prepare a waffle batter as shown on page 134, replacing the all-purpose flour with spelt flour. Cook waffles in a greased waffle iron. Wash and pit generous 1lb (500 g) cherries. Bring to a boil in a pan with a scant 7 tablespoons (100 ml) water and 1 tablespoon Kirsch.

Preparation time: 20 minutes

... with sorbet
Prepare a waffle batter as shown on page 134. Cook waffles in a greased waffle iron. Serve with frozen sorbet and fruit.

Preparation time: 30 minutes

... with plum compote
Prepare a waffle batter, replacing the all-purpose flour with wholemeal flour. Cook waffles in a waffle iron. Wash and pit 11 oz (300 g) plums. In a pan, bring to a boil 7 tablespoons (100 ml) red wine, 1 cinnamon stick, 1 pinch star anise, and a scant 1 cup (200 g) sugar. Add the plums and stew for 10 minutes, until soft.

Preparation time: 30 minutes

... with chocolate sauce
Prepare a waffle batter (see page 134). Add $3\frac{1}{2}$ oz (100 g) toasted and chopped sunflower seeds and 1 teaspoon lemon juice. Cook waffles in a greased waffle iron. In a pan, bring to a boil a generous $\frac{3}{4}$ cup (200 ml) water and 2 tablespoons sugar. Finely chop 6 oz (175 g) dark chocolate and melt in the sugar mixture. Serve waffles with the chocolate sauce and 1 tablespoon toasted sunflower seeds.

SAUCES
for waffles

Try serving waffles with a fruit sauce, sorbet, or a velvety vanilla or cinnamon cream.

Preparation time: 30 minutes

... with apple sauce

Prepare a waffle batter using 1$^1/_3$ cups (200 g) flour and $^1/_3$ cup (50 g) cornmeal. Cook waffles in a waffle iron. Peel, core, and dice 4 apples, and place in a pan with 2 tablespoons lemon juice and 2 tablespoons sugar. Add generous $^3/_4$ cup (200 ml) water. Bring to a boil, then reduce the heat and simmer for 20 minutes. Add sugar and cinnamon to taste.

Preparation time: 30 minutes

... with baked banana

Prepare a waffle batter as shown on page 134, using a scant 1 cup (125 g) each flour and ground almonds. Cook waffles in a greased waffle iron. Peel and halve 4 bananas. Cook in 3 table-spoons butter in a pan, until golden brown on both sides. Serve with 1 tablespoon liquid honey and chopped almonds.

Mango sauce

Peel and pit a mango, and purée the flesh in a blender with orange liqueur. Add sugar to taste.

Raspberry sorbet

Pulse frozen raspberries in a blender, and add sugar to taste.

Vanilla or cinnamon cream

Whisk heavy whipping cream until stiff, and add vanilla sugar or cinnamon to taste.

CHOCOLATE MOUSSE
with dark chocolate

Serves 4

12 oz (350 g)	dark chocolate, or couverture
3 tbsp	milk
3 tbsp	butter
6	eggs
3 tbsp	granulated sugar
20 min.	preparation time

Step by step

Coarsely chop the chocolate or couverture.

Separate the eggs. Mix the egg yolks with the sugar, and stir into the chocolate mixture.

Heat the milk in a pan and dissolve the chopped chocolate, stirring continuously.

Beat the egg whites until stiff and fold into the mousse.

Melt the butter in a small pan, and stir into the chocolate mixture.

Spoon the mousse into bowls and chill in the icebox.

CHOCOLATE INFO

Who can resist the sweet seduction of velvety **chocolate**? From simple milk and bittersweet chocolate through the finest,

dark varieties, these days it comes in almost every imaginable flavor, including chile, pepper, and nutmeg.

The raw material used to make chocolate is cocoa powder. Contrary to popular belief, the beans that are ground into powder are not sweet, but very bitter. In fact, chocolate is only sweet when sugar is added to it. Found inside pods that grow on cocoa trees, the purple-colored cocoa beans are fermented, dried, and roasted. The shells are opened by high pressure, the beans crushed to cocoa mass, and up to 20% of the cocoa butter removed. This creates a paste, which is ground into cocoa powder.

Cocoa mass is mixed with cocoa butter and sugar in varying quantities to make different types of chocolate—the higher the content of original cocoa butter, the better quality the chocolate. For this complex process, chocolate manufacturers use machines called "conches" to mix the heated mass until smooth.

139

SAUCES
for mousse

Fruit sauces are quick to prepare, and also go very well with ice cream.

Kiwi sauce
Peel and purée kiwi fruit. Mix with sugar and lemon juice, and fold in peppermint liqueur. Perfect with a light fruit mousse.

Cherry sauce
Bring to a boil pitted Morello cherries, sugar, grated lemon rind, cinnamon, and cherry juice. Thicken with cornstarch. Perfect with coffee, poppy seed, and coconut and yogurt mousse.

Berry sauce
Bring to a boil mixed, thawed frozen berries in a little water. Purée, and press through a sieve. Fold in confectioners' sugar and chopped pine nuts.

MOUSSE
several

Mousse has a wonderful, light, and airy texture. With countless varieties to choose from, this classic dessert of French cuisine enjoys worldwide popularity. Mousse is much lighter and fluffier than other desserts, and more like foam. Although quick to prepare, it does need to be refrigerated for several

Preparation time: 20 minutes

... with apricots
Beat 3 egg yolks and 5 tablespoons sugar until fluffy. Purée 7 oz (200 g) pitted apricots with $^2/_3$ cup (150 ml) apricot juice, and press through a sieve. Heat 1 cup (250 ml) of the mixture with 3 soaked gelatin leaves. Add the egg and sugar mixture. Fold in 1 cup (250 ml) light whipping cream, stiffly whisked. Add liqueur to taste, and chill in the icebox.

Preparation time: 30 minutes

... with coffee
Soak 4 gelatin leaves in a little water. Heat 7 tablespoons (100 ml) cooled espresso with 5 tablespoons sugar and the squeezed gelatin, and stir until smooth. Fold in 4$^1/_2$ oz (125 g) Mascarpone and leave to cool. Just before the mousse starts to thicken, fold in a generous $^3/_4$ cup (200 ml) light whipping cream, stiffly whisked. Chill in the icebox.

variations

hours. Mousse creations are endless—try white chocolate, coffee, or liqueur; coconut, peppermint, or cognac... and add a delicious sauce or cream for the ultimate dream dessert! Here are four variations for you to try out.

Preparation time: 20 minutes

... with coconut and yogurt

Soak 2 white gelatin leaves in water. Mix together 1 cup (250 ml) creamy yogurt, 5 tablespoons milk, 3 tablespoons confectioners' sugar, and 4 tablespoons canned coconut cream. Dissolve the squeezed gelatin in a little hot water, stirring continuously. Add to the coconut mixture. Fold in 1 1/4 cups (300 ml) light whipping cream, stiffly whisked, and chill in the icebox.

Preparation time: 15 minutes

... with poppy seeds

Mix 4 tablespoons cornstarch, 1 egg yolk, and 2 tablespoons milk. Bring to a boil 2 cups (475 ml) milk with 3 tablespoons confectioners' sugar, 1 pinch salt, and 3 tablespoons vanilla sugar. Combine with the cornstarch mixture and bring to a boil, stirring continuously. Add 5 tablespoons ground poppy seeds and boil again. Beat 1 egg white until stiff, and fold in. Leave to cool.

SAUCES
for mousse

These three sauces taste delicious with cookies as well as mousse.

Cream and raspberry sauce

Bring to a boil light cream, saffron, and lemon zest. Stir in vanilla custard sauce powder, sugar, and raspberry liqueur. Perfect with poppy seed mousse.

Chocolate sauce

Chop dark chocolate and melt in hot light cream, stirring continuously. Perfect with coconut and yogurt mousse.

Nougat sauce

Finely chop nougat and melt in 2/3 cup (150 ml) chocolate sauce. Perfect with any light mousse.

FRUIT SALAD
with melon and strawberries

INFO

Cantaloupe belongs to the muskmelon family. Due to its warty skin, the Germans also give it the name "Warzenmelone," which translates literally as "wart melon." The more appealing name "cantaloupe" originates from a summer residence of the Pope, in Cantalupo, Italy. Here, melons were cultivated early on, due to their popular taste. Their orange flesh is very high in vitamins and fiber and low in calories, despite its sugar content. Cantaloupe is particularly tasty when eaten ice cold.

Serves 4

6	*apricots*
2	*peaches*
1	*cantaloupe melon*
2	*apples*
1	*pear*
9 oz (250 g)	*strawberries*
7 tbsp (100ml)	*apple juice*
1 tbsp	*honey*
	slivered almonds, mint
20 min.	*preparation time*

Step by step

Wash and pit the apricots and peaches. Cut into cubes.

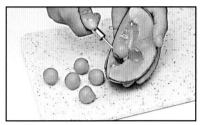

Peel the cantaloupe, remove the seeds, and scoop out the flesh with a melon baller.

Peel and core the apples and pear. Cut into cubes.

Clean and wash the strawberries, pat dry, and cut in half.

Mix the fruit with 7 tablespoons (100 ml) of apple juice and 1 tablespoon of honey. Garnish with slivered almonds and mint.

Side dish

Chocolate muffins: beat $^1/_2$ cup (110 g) softened butter, 7 tablespoons (100 g) sugar, 2 eggs, $^3/_4$ cup (170 ml) milk, and 3 tablespoons vanilla sugar until fluffy. Mix $1^3/_4$ cups (250 g) flour with 1 oz (30 g) cocoa powder, 2 teaspoons baking soda, and 1 pinch salt, and stir well. Fold in $3^1/_2$ oz (100 g) grated dark chocolate. Divide the mixture between 12 greased muffin molds. Bake in the oven at 325 °F/160 °C for 15 minutes.

Dip

Mascarpone cream: beat 2 egg yolks and 4 tablespoons confectioners' sugar until fluffy. Fold in 9 oz (250 g) Mascarpone and 7 tablespoons (100 ml) light whipping cream, stiffly whisked. Beat the egg white until stiff and fold into the cream mixture.

DESSERTS

SIDE DISHES
for fruit salad

If fruit salad on its own isn't quite enough, try adding rice pudding, crispy semolina slices, or muesli.

Rice pudding

Prepare 1¼ cups (250 g) round-grain rice according to the pack instructions. Sprinkle with cinnamon and sugar. Perfect with exotic fruit, and fruit salad with grapes.

Semolina slices

Prepare semolina according to the pack instructions, and spread over a greased baking sheet. Sprinkle with butter and chopped nuts. Bake in a pre-heated oven for 4–5 minutes and cut into slices.

Muesli

Mix together different cereals with raisins and sunflower seeds. Add sugar to taste. Perfect with all recipe variations.

Preparation time: 20 minutes

... with exotic fruit

Deseed 7 oz (200 g) litchi. Slice 1 star fruit. Cut 4 figs into eighths. Cut the flesh of 4 kiwis and 1 mango into cubes, and dice 3½ oz (100 g) papaya. Peel and dice ½ baby pineapple. Mix fruit with 6 tablespoons (50 g) toasted sunflower seeds and 2 tablespoons orange juice. Add sugar.

Preparation time: 25 minutes

... with cherries, amarettini, and cream

Wash and pit 11 oz (300 g) cherries. Sprinkle with 2 tablespoons grappa, and leave to soak. Mix with 7 oz (200 g) diced mango. Place 7 oz (200 g) amarettini macaroons in a plastic bag. Crush with a rolling pin, and mix with the fruit. Whisk 1 cup (250 ml) light whipping cream until stiff, and fold in. Spoon into glasses and sprinkle with roasted, chopped pistachios.

FRUIT SALAD
several variations

Summer brings a wealth of fresh fruit to our tables. A main meal can even be replaced by a fruit salad. Try adding Ricotta, yogurt, or zabaglione—whichever you prefer.

Preparation time: 15 minutes

... with Ricotta and honey

Wash, dry, and halve 9 oz (250 g) strawberries. Mix with 9 oz (250 g) washed blackberries, 2 tablespoons lemon juice, and 2 tablespoons confectioners' sugar. Beat 14 oz (400 g) Ricotta, 3 tablespoons honey, and a scant 7 tablespoons (100 ml) light whipping cream, until smooth. Place alternate layers of the Ricotta mixture and berries in glasses. Garnish with mint leaves.

Preparation time: 25 minutes

... with berries and zabaglione

Combine 9 oz (250 g) mixed berries (redcurrants, raspberries, and blueberries) with 1 tablespoon sugar and the juice of one lemon. Chill in the icebox. Beat 4 egg yolks, 3 tablespoons sugar, and grated lemon rind in a bain-marie until creamy. Gradually stir in 4 tablespoons Marsala. Serve with the berries.

Preparation time: 25 minutes

... with vanilla yogurt and chocolate flakes

Slice 3 bananas. Mix with 2 chopped oranges, 2 diced kiwis, and $3^1/_2$ oz (100 g) diced pineapple. Pour over 3 tablespoons pineapple juice. Add 1 cup (250 ml) yogurt, 3 tablespoons vanilla sugar, and $1^3/_4$ oz (50 g) finely chopped dark chocolate. Sprinkle with toasted coconut flakes.

Preparation time: 20 minutes

... with grapes and toasted nuts

Mix together 9 oz (250 g) each black and white grapes, and 2 each pitted and diced peaches and nectarines. Add 3 tablespoons acacia honey, 1 tablespoon chestnut spread, and the juice of one lemon. Fold in $3^1/_2$ oz (100 g) toasted walnuts. Sprinkle with coarse sugar.

SPONGE INFO

Sponge is made from a very light, airy batter. It is used to make sponge cakes, which can be flavored in many different ways,

and also for flan cases and jelly roll cakes. The secret of the texture lies in preparing a foamy mixture, since the egg yolk and sugar need to be beaten until fluffy before folding in the flour. The sponge rises mainly because of the air whipped into the egg whites, so it is also important to ensure that they are stiffly beaten before being added to the mixture. The cake is then baked in the oven.

FLAN GLAZE INFO

Flan glaze is the jelly-like substance that is used to cover the top of fruit flans and fruit slices. The main ingredient is a gelling agent such as ground gelatin, pectin, locust bean gum, or carrageenan. Glazes also

contain acidity regulators and colorings: for example, to create a red glaze.

Serves 12

1	*sponge flan case (ready-made)*
3 tbsp	*cornstarch*
9 oz (250 g)	*Mascarpone*
3 tbsp	*sugar*
1³/₄ lb (750 g)	*strawberries*
1 cup (250 ml)	*grape juice*
1 pack.	*red flan glaze*
2 tbsp	*chopped, toasted hazelnuts*
25 min.	*preparation time*

Step by step

Sprinkle the flan case with cornstarch.

Arrange the strawberries over the layer of Mascarpone.

Mix the Mascarpone with 1 tablespoon of sugar, and spread over the flan case.

Prepare a glaze from the grape juice, the remaining sugar, and glaze powder. Spoon over the strawberries.

Wash the strawberries, remove the stalks, pat dry, and cut into halves.

Sprinkle the cooled glaze with chopped nuts.

QUICK AND EASY FLAN
with strawberries and nuts

DESSERTS

DRINKS
for flan

The flans shown here are so quick to prepare, you'll have plenty of time to create an elegant drink as well.

Hot chocolate
Mix together cocoa powder, hot milk, and sugar. Melt chopped chocolate in hot milk. Mix the two drinks, and serve with cinnamon sticks.

Irish coffee
Mix together strong coffee with sugar and whiskey. Top with whipped cream.

Latte macchiato
Pour frothed milk into glasses, and leave to stand for 2 minutes. Carefully pour 1 cup espresso into each, and sprinkle with cocoa powder.

QUICK AND
several

Flans are so quick and easy to make, even when visitors are already on their way. And it doesn't have to mean reaching into the cupboard for a ready-made case and filling it with canned fruit, either. Puff pastry is quick, too, and tastes absolutely heavenly in Tarte Tatin. Equally tasty are flans prepared with

Preparation time: 25 minutes

... with cookies, chocolate, and Mascarpone cream
Crush 10 amaretti macaroons with a rolling pin. Combine with 2 whisked egg whites and place in a dish. Bake at 350 °F/180 °C for 10 minutes. Mix 8 oz (225 g) Mascarpone with 1 tablespoon lemon juice, 2 tablespoons sugar, and $3^1/_2$ oz (100 g) finely chopped chocolate. Spread over the flan case, and sprinkle with toasted almonds.

Preparation time: 25 minutes

... with spongecake fingers, pineapple, and banana
Mix 7 tablespoons (100 g) softened butter with 7 oz (200 g) crumbled spongecake fingers, and use to line a springform pan. Peel 1 banana and 2 kiwis, cut into slices, and spread over the base. Mix 1 cup (250 ml) heavy sour cream with 3 tablespoons vanilla sugar and 3 gelatin leaves dissolved in pineapple juice, then spread over the fruit. Top with pineapple slices filled with redcurrants.

EASY FLAN
variations

crumbled cookies or sponge fingers, creating a base in no time at all. Let your imagination run wild! Here are a few tasty ideas for quick and easy flans.

Preparation time: 30 minutes

... with puff pastry, cherries, and cream

Roll out chilled puff pastry to fit a greased and lined springform pan (9 in. / 22 cm). Arrange 14 oz (400 g) drained, canned cherries over the top. Bake in the oven at 400 °F/200 °C for about 20 minutes. Beat 1 cup (250 ml) heavy whipping cream until stiff. Spread over the cherries and sprinkle with 3 tablespoons Advocaat.

Preparation time: 30 minutes

... with apple, nuts, and cinnamon

Mix ²/₃ cup (150 g) sugar and 3¹/₂ tablespoons (50 g) butter in a pie plate. Arrange 4 peeled and cored apples on top, cut into slices. Sprinkle with 2 tablespoons chopped nuts, cinnamon, and sugar and 2 tablespoons flaked butter. Roll out chilled puff pastry and place on top of the apples. Bake at 400 °F/200 °C for 20 minutes, then turn out.

DRINKS
for flan

If you want to serve something special to drink with your flan, here are three suggestions. Try one, but watch out... you might want another!

Mexican chocolate

Mix cocoa powder, sugar, salt, and chile flakes in a little warm milk in a pan. Add milk, and bring to a boil. Beat with a whisk until creamy, pour into glasses, and add espresso.

Irish cream

Beat heavy cream and coffee powder until fluffy. Beat eggs with whiskey until creamy. Mix the two together with hot milk, a little coffee liqueur, and sugar.

Coffee with Advocaat

Pour a small quantity of Advocaat into coffee cups and add hot coffee. Garnish with whipped cream and chocolate flakes.

QUARK

with kiwi, orange and banana

INFO

Vanilla sugar is conventional granulated sugar that has been enriched with true natural vanilla. Vanillin sugar, on the other hand, is flavored with artificially-made vanillin, which is supposed to recreate the true vanilla flavor. You can make your own vanilla sugar by combining 1 scraped vanilla bean with granulated sugar and sealing it in an airtight jar. The sugar soon absorbs the vanilla flavor.

Serves 4

14 oz (400 g)	low-fat quark
7 tbsp (100 ml)	yogurt
3 tbsp	vanilla sugar
7 tbsp (100 ml)	light whipping cream
1 tbsp	rum
3	kiwis
4	bananas
2	oranges
2 tbsp	lemon juice
2 tbsp	sugar
15 min.	preparation time

Step by step

Mix the quark with the yogurt and vanilla sugar.

Beat the cream until stiff, then fold into the quark mixture with the rum.

Peel and dice the kiwis. Peel the bananas and cut into slices.

Peel and deseed the oranges, then slice and cube them.

Combine the fruit with the lemon juice and sugar, add to the quark mixture, and spoon into glasses.

Side dish

Chocolate crêpes: prepare a batter using 9 tablespoons (80 g) flour, 1 tablespoon cocoa powder, 3 tablespoons sugar, 2 eggs, $^3/_4$ cup (175 ml) milk, and 2 tablespoons melted butter, and leave to stand for 15 minutes. Cook crêpes in a greased crêpe pan, or small (6-in./15-cm) omelet pan. Sprinkle with confectioners' sugar.

Dip

Coconut and pineapple cream: scrape out the flesh of $^1/_4$ coconut, pour over 7 tablespoons (100 ml) hot water, and leave to soak for 15 minutes. Press through a sieve lined with muslin, and squeeze well. Mix in coconut milk, 1 tablespoon lemon juice, 1 tablespoon sugar, 2 tablespoons white rum, and $3^1/_2$ oz (100 g) puréed pineapple.

QUARK

several variations

Quark as a dessert? You may not think it sounds very exciting. But look again—or, rather, have a taste, and you'll soon change your mind! Liven up quark / Mascarpone / Ricotta desserts with just a few special ingredients.

Preparation time: 25 minutes

... with baked pineapple and coconut

Mix 12 oz (350 g) Ricotta, 2 tablespoons Cointreau, 2 tablespoons sugar, and 1 teaspoon grated lemon rind. Beat $^2/_3$ cup (150 ml) heavy cream until almost stiff and fold in. Dice $^1/_2$ pineapple. Sprinkle with 2 tablespoons coconut flakes, and bake in the oven for 10 minutes. Mix 7 tablespoons melted butter with 4 tablespoons honey, and sprinkle over the fruit.

Preparation time: 25 minutes

... with exotic fruit and cashews

Purée the flesh of $^1/_2$ mango with 1 tablespoon honey, and mix with 14 oz (400 g) quark and 7 tablespoons (100 ml) yogurt. Peel and dice 1 kiwi. Peel 1 guava, and cut into cubes. Deseed 1 pomegranate. Dice $^1/_4$ papaya. Divide the mango quark into bowls, arrange the fruit on top, drizzle with 2 tablespoons coconut liqueur, and sprinkle with chopped cashews.

Preparation time: 30 minutes

... with vanilla, cinnamon, and cherries

Mix together 14 oz (400 g) low-fat quark, 7 tablespoons (100 ml) each yogurt and stiffly whisked light whipping cream, and 3 tablespoons vanilla sugar. Pit 9 oz (250 g) cherries and bring to a boil in a pan with 7 tablespoons (100 ml) each red wine and water, 2 tablespoons sugar, and cinnamon. Reduce the heat, and simmer for 5 minutes. Thicken and leave to cool. Serve with the vanilla quark.

Preparation time: 20 minutes

... with mixed berries and cantucci

Sort and wash 11 oz (300 g) mixed berries (e.g. blackberries, raspberries, blueberries, redcurrants) and remove the stems. Mix 14 oz (400 g) quark, 1 tablespoon grappa, and 2 tablespoons sugar. Crush 9 oz (250 g) cantucci cookies, and divide into bowls. Top with berries and quark. Garnish with slivered almonds.

SIDE DISHES
for quark

Here are some other tasty treats to serve with quark dishes:

Chocolate lattices
Melt couverture. Cut out a small corner of a plastic food bag, fill with couverture, and "draw" lattices on parchment paper. Leave to cool. Remove carefully. Perfect with all recipe variations.

French toast
Place slices of bread in a dish, pour over a batter made from eggs, sugar, and milk, and leave to soak. Cook until crispy in hot clarified butter. Perfect with the baked pineapple, and vanilla with cherries variations.

Cherry beignets
Prepare a batter using egg yolk, flour, white wine, sugar, and salt, and leave to stand for 15 minutes. Fold in beaten egg whites. Dip sweet cherries with their stems into the batter (5 cherries tied together) and cook in hot fat. Perfect with the baked pineapple, Mascarpone and sponge, and chocolate pieces recipe variations.

Preparation time: 20 minutes

... with Mascarpone and sponge
Line a dish with spongecake fingers, and drizzle with cold espresso and 2 tablespoons Amaretto. Mix together 3 egg yolks, 3 tablespoons sugar, and a generous 1lb (500 g) Mascarpone. Spread $1/2$ the Mascarpone cream over the sponge, place another layer of sponge on top, and finish with the cream. Sprinkle with cocoa powder. Chill in the icebox.

Preparation time: 20 minutes

... with chocolate pieces and mint
Mix together 14 oz (400 g) Mascarpone, 7 oz (200 g) Ricotta, 1 egg, 2 tablespoons sugar, and 2 tablespoons peppermint liqueur. Finely chop $1^3/_4$ oz (50 g) each dark chocolate and white chocolate, and fold into the quark with $1^3/_4$ oz (50 g) raisins soaked in rum. Spoon the mixture into bowls. Garnish with raspberries and mint leaves.

PANCAKES
with apples

	Serves 4
2¹/₂ cups (350 g)	*all-purpose flour*
5 tbsp	*sugar*
1 pinch	*salt*
4	*eggs*
2 cups (500 ml)	*milk*
4	*apples*
3 tbsp	*butter*
	Confectioners' sugar
30 min.	*preparation time*

Step by step

Mix the flour, sugar, salt, and eggs in a bowl.

Heat the butter in a skillet. Add half the batter, and cook.

Slowly beat in the milk. Leave the batter to stand for 20 minutes.

Arrange some apple slices on top. Cover, and cook for 3 minutes.

Peel and core the apples, and cut them into thin slices.

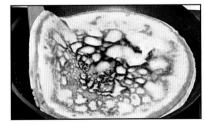

Flip the pancake, and cook for another 3 minutes. Repeat the process with the rest of the batter and apples. Sprinkle with confectioners' sugar to serve.

MILK INFO

Not only is **cow's milk** extremely popular and drunk in vast quantities, it is also the basis of many products such as yogurt, cheese, and quark.

Unfortunately, many people are lactose (milk sugar) intolerant; they cannot digest it, to varying degrees, and therefore have to limit their intake of milk and cream, or even avoid it completely. Milk is an important source of calcium, protein, vitamins, and minerals. Commercially available milk is heat treated to give it a longer shelf life, while untreated raw or attested milk and raw milk products can only be obtained from farmers.

EGGS INFO

Eggs are a source of valuable protein; they have little fat, and virtually no carbohydrates. The yolk contains a wealth of vitamins (excluding vitamin C), iron, and lots of minerals. Eggs are a fundamental ingredient in many dishes, and a kitchen would not be a kitchen without them. The only downside is that their cholesterol content is relatively high. The grading system for eggs in America is based on the appearance of a chicken's egg and the quality of its albumen and yolk; grade AA is the highest, followed by grade A, and then grade B.

SIDE DISHES
for pancakes

Mouth-watering pancakes taste best with a cream and/or fruit topping.

Fruit cream

Beat $^2/_3$ cup (150 ml) light whipping cream and 4 tablespoons confectioners' sugar until stiff. Fold in 4 tablespoons heavy sour cream. Peel 1 orange (or another kind of fruit), deseed, and chop finely. Sprinkle with 2 tablespoons orange liqueur. Perfect with the pancakes with hazelnut cream, and pancakes with stewed plums.

Berry salad

Sort and wash 9 oz (250 g) raspberries, $5^1/_2$ oz (150 g) blackberries, $3^1/_2$ oz (100 g) blueberries, and $5^1/_2$ oz (150 g) each redcurrants and blackcurrants. Pull the redcurrants and blackcurrants from their stems and purée with 2 tablespoons elderberry jelly. Press through a sieve, and mix with 4 tablespoons crème de cassis. Mix with the remaining fruit. Perfect with blueberry pancakes, and pancakes with hazelnut cream.

PANCAKES
several

Pancakes are a huge hit with children. They're not alone, as a lot of adult food lovers swear by them as a simple and tasty meal. They can be served with a variety of toppings or fillings. Beside the classic apple sauce, they can be combined with almost any kind of fruit, whether fresh or stewed in a compote.

Preparation time: 20 minutes

... with blueberries

Prepare a batter using 7 oz (200 g) flour, 7 tablespoons (100 ml) milk, 4 egg yolks, and 1 pinch salt. Beat 4 egg whites until stiff, and fold in. Heat 2 tablespoons clarified butter in a skillet, pour in the batter mix, then top with 11 oz (300 g) blueberries. Cook, then flip over and cook the other side. Sprinkle with sugar to serve.

Preparation time: 30 minutes

... with stewed plums

Prepare a batter as shown on page 154, folding in $3^1/_2$ oz (100 g) raisins. Simmer 14 oz (400 g) pitted plums with red wine, cinnamon, and sugar for 10 minutes. Cook pancakes in 2 tablespoons butter. Turn and cook on the other side. Tear into pieces using two forks and cook for a little longer. Dust with confectioners' sugar and serve with the plums.

SIDE DISHES
for pancakes

variations

Try adding chocolate for the ultimate taste experience. Or, for those who prefer a more savory pancake, a pancake pizza with salami, cheese, or tuna is delicious. And here are a few suggestions for the more sweet-toothed among you.

Try these two fruit dishes with pancakes, instead of strawberries or stewed plums.

Preparation time: 30 minutes

... with hazelnut cream

Prepare a batter as shown on page 154, using 11 oz (300 g) flour and $^2/_3$ cup (50 g) ground hazelnuts. Cook pancakes. Spread each pancake with hazelnut cream, made from whisked heavy whipping cream mixed with chopped hazelnuts.

Red wine cherries

Caramelize 2 tablespoons sugar in a pan, stirring continuously. Stir in 3 tablespoons red wine and reduce. Add generous 1lb (500 g) Morello cherries (from a jar) with 3 tablespoons of the juice. Bring to a boil. Mix 1 teaspoon cornstarch in a little Kirsch, and use to thicken the sauce.

Preparation time: 30 minutes

... flambéed with fresh strawberries

Prepare a batter as shown on page 154, stirring in 3 tablespoons dried coconut. Cook pancakes, remove from the pan, and keep warm. Wash and halve generous 1lb (500 g) strawberries, then mix with 1 tablespoon sugar. Purée half the strawberries. Place pancakes in the pan, sprinkle with orange liqueur, and set alight. Serve immediately, with strawberry sauce and fresh strawberries.

Pear compote

Peel and core 4 pears, cut into slices, and sprinkle with 2 tablespoons lemon juice. Bring to a boil 1$^1/_2$ cups (350 ml) white wine, 5 tablespoons sugar, 1 vanilla bean, and 1 teaspoon grated lemon rind. Simmer for 2 minutes, add to the pears, cover, and poach for 3 minutes. Remove the fruit and vanilla bean with a slotted spoon, and reduce for 10 minutes to a syrup. Add pear brandy to taste. Pour over the pears, and sprinkle with toasted pine nuts.

Index of recipes

BREADED SCHNITZEL 92–95
... Viennese style
... with a herb coating
... stuffed with prunes
... with an almond coating
... with a chile coating

CARPACCIO 24–27
... with beef and Parmesan
... with veal and capers
... with tuna and lime dressing
... with turkey breast and roasted pine nuts
... with salmon and horseradish cream

CHOCOLATE MOUSSE 138–141
... with dark chocolate
... with apricots
... with coconut and yogurt
... with coffee
... with poppy seeds

COLD VEGETABLE SOUP 56–59
... with bell pepper, tomato, and cucumber
... with beets and crème fraîche
... with cucumber, celery, and cress
... with almonds and garlic
... with tomatoes and garlic croutons

CREAMY SOUP 36–39
... with tomato and goat's cheese
... with asparagus and ham
... with zucchini and croutons
... with pumpkin and roasted pumpkin seeds
... with fresh herbs and cream
... with carrot, orange, and ginger
... with herby cream cheese and white wine

CROSTINI 40–43
... with tomatoes and garlic
... with mushroom cream
... with chicken livers and capers
... with eggplant purée
... with anchovy cream and mozzarella

CURRY 108–111
... with beef and bell peppers
... with pork, bamboo shoots, and tomatoes
... with chicken, apple, and mint
... with fish and potatoes
... with lamb, apricots, and peanuts

FILLED BAGUETTE 32–35
... with chicken breast and salad
... with roast beef and vegetables
... with Parma ham, Camembert, and peach
... with Bündenfleisch, pear, and cress
... with cream cheese, salmon, and radish sprouts

FRIED RICE 74–77
... with zucchini and bell pepper
... with ground meat and mixed vegetables
... with wok vegetables
... with turkey, almonds, and raisins
... with Chinese mushrooms and ginger

FRUIT SALAD 142–145
... with melon and strawberries
... with exotic fruit
... with Ricotta and honey
... with vanilla yogurt and chocolate flakes
... with cherries, amarettini, and cream
... with berries and zabaglione
... with grapes and toasted nuts

GRILLED SKEWERS 20–23
... with marinated chicken breast
... with chicken, chile, and mushrooms
... with shrimp, garlic, and lemongrass
... with pork and scallions
... with fish, cherry tomatoes, and zucchini
... with turkey breast, artichokes, and olives
... with mixed vegetables

MEATBALLS 100–103
... with tomato sauce
... with onion sauce
... filled with ewe's milk cheese
... with onions and bell peppers
... with ginger and soy
... with a sesame crust
... with fried egg

MEAT STRIPS 124–127
... with mushrooms and beet (beef stroganoff)
... with liver and apples
... with duck and bell peppers
... with spicy sausage and cheese
... with veal and mushrooms

MINUTE SIRLOINS 128–131
... with herb butter
... with red wine and peppercorn sauce
... with dried fruit
... with mushrooms and onion
... with olive and anchovy butter
... with cherry tomatoes and arugula
... with a cheese and herb crust

MIXED SALAD 52–55
... with arugula, nuts, and Parmesan
... with duck breast and orange slices
... with fried pike perch and sprouts
... with bacon and goat's cheese baguette
... with vegetables and Feta
... with mushrooms, Parmesan, and garlic croutons
... with cabbage, dates, and apple

OMELET 44–47
... with mixed vegetables
... with fried chanterelles and herbs
... with ewe's milk cheese and tomato
... with potato, bacon, and bell pepper
... with red onion, garlic, and shrimp
... with scallions, bell pepper, and cilantro
... with chile, red beans, and cheese

PANCAKE ROLLS 28–31
... with spinach and cream cheese
... with salmon and sour cream
... with tuna cream and salad
... with boiled ham and cheese
... with asparagus and Parma ham
... with bacon, goat's cheese, and maple syrup
... with ewe's milk cheese, tomatoes, and cucumber

PANCAKES 154–157
... with apples
... with blueberries
... with hazelnut cream
... with stewed plums
... flambéed with fresh strawberries

PAN-COOKED VEGETABLES 78–81
... with almonds
... with bell pepper and beef strips
... with cellophane noodles, sugar snap peas, and carrots
... with broccoli, mushrooms, and zucchini
... with bok choy, sprouts, and shrimp
... with white cabbage, ground meat, and onions
... with leek, nuts, and tofu

PAN-FRIED FISH 112–115
... with mixed vegetables
... with Parma ham and carrots
... with olives, broccoli, and cherry tomatoes
... with ratatouille vegetables
... with spinach and chickpeas
... with celery, pineapple, and sprouts
... with seafood

PASTA 62–69
... with ham and cream sauce
... with venison and mushrooms
... with shrimp and cherry tomatoes
... with goat's cheese and arugula
... with green spring vegetables
... with salmon and cream sauce
... with morels and truffle oil
... with pesto
... with garlic and oil
... with red pesto
... with butter and Parmesan
... with spinach and chile

POACHED FISH 120–123
... with mustard and cream sauce
... with an Asian marinade on vegetables
... with pistachio and Parmesan cream
... with wine cream
... with vegetable vinaigrette
... with cucumber
... with herbs and béchamel sauce

POTATOES IN THEIR SKINS 86–89
... with herbed quark
... with eggs and green sauce
... with roast meat, gherkins, and egg
... with bacon and meatloaf
... au gratin
... goulash potatoes
... wrapped in bacon

POULTRY 116–119
... with herbs and cherry tomatoes
... with capers and lemons
... with a herb and mustard crust
... au gratin, with ham
... with vegetable salad

QUARK 150–153
... with kiwi, orange, and banana
... with baked pineapple and coconut
... with vanilla, cinnamon, and cherries
... with Mascarpone and sponge
... with exotic fruit and cashews
... with mixed berries and cantucci
... with chocolate pieces and mint

QUICK AND EASY FLAN 146–149
... with strawberries and nuts
... with cookies, chocolate, and Mascarpone cream
... with puff pastry, cherries, and cream
... with spongecake fingers, pineapple, and banana
... with apple, nuts, and cinnamon

QUICK PIZZA 82–85
... with tomato and mozzarella
... with Serrano ham and Gorgonzola
... with goat's cheese, pears, and honey
... with artichokes and olives
... with tuna and onions

RISOTTO 70–73
... with peas ("risi e bisi")
... with radicchio and Parmesan
... with bolete mushrooms
... with pumpkin
... with saffron and butter
... with fennel
... with white and green asparagus

SCHNITZEL 96–99
... with ham and sage
... with thyme and capers
... with Gorgonzola sauce
... with orange sauce
... with sherry sauce
... with spicy sauce
... with cherry sauce

TOASTED SANDWICH 48–51
... with cheese and ham
... with cured beef, avocado, and Brie
... with peaches, goat's cheese, and radicchio
... with mozzarella, Parma ham, and tomatoes
... with chicken breast, mango, and cheese

WAFFLES 134–137
... with cinnamon and sugar
... with hot cherries
... with sorbet
... with apple sauce
... with plum compote
... with chocolate sauce
... with baked banana

WOK DISHES 104–107
... with sweet and sour sauce
... with beef and lemongrass
... with chicken and bamboo shoots
... with fish, papaya, and chile
... with omelet, rice noodles, and cilantro
... with sugar snap peas, broccoli, and carrots
... with pork, sprouts, and shiitake mushrooms

Index of recipes

Side dishes

Aromatic rice 105
Baked pumpkin 119
Berry salad 156
Braised mushrooms 113
Bunched carrots 121
Buttered potatoes 114
Cheese canapés 58
Cherry beignets 153
Chicken and grape skewers 59
Chocolate crêpes 151
Chocolate lattices 153
Chocolate muffins 143
Cilantro rice 81
Coconut rice 110
Couscous 81
Croquette potatoes 99
Djuvec rice 81
Duchess potatoes 99
Egg noodles 127
French fries 129
French toast 153
Fried bacon 71
Fried cherry tomatoes 95
Fried chicken drumsticks 72
Fried mini dumplings 39
Fried potatoes 93, 118
Fried prawns 53
Fried rice noodles 107
Fried rice 107
Fried sardines 72
Fruit cream 156
Garlic baguette 114
Garlic bread 37, 79
Grilled vegetable skewers 59
Herb pasta 113
Herb rice 110
Lamb chops 72
Lemon rice 110
Lentil purée (dhal) 111
Mango pasta 119
Marinated eggplant 76
Marinated mushrooms 77
Marinated onions 77
Marinated zucchini 76
Mashed potato 99
Mashed sweet potato 118
Meatballs 87
Mixed mushrooms 95
Muesli 144
Parsley potatoes 101
Pear compote 157
Polenta 126
Polenta pieces 79
Potato and celery mash 126
Raita (cucumber yogurt) 111
Red wine cherries 157
Rice balls 39
Rice noodles 107
Rice pudding 144
Rice with spinach and peas 121
Saffron rice 127
Salmon canapés 58
Salmon tartare 29
Sausage and cheese skewers 59
Sausage meatballs 37
Sautéed cucumbers 111
Semolina slices 144

Spicy potatoes 118
Strawberries with mint 135
Sweet corn and leek 119
Swiss rösti 126
Tartare canapés 58
Tomato rice 114
Vegetable skewers 87
Wholemeal croutons 39
Wild rice 127
Wilted spinach 95

Dips, dressings, sauces, and spreads

Aïoli 53
Almond and parsley pesto 68
Aniseed sauce 123
Avocado cream 43
Bell pepper sauce 69
Berry sauce 140
Broccoli sauce 69
Cherry sauce 140
Chervil cream 88
Chile dip 105
Chocolate sauce 141
Coconut and pineapple cream 151
Corn and chile relish 46
Cranberry cream 35
Cream and raspberry sauce 141
Cream cheese spread 35, 43
Cucumber and tomato raita 46
Curry sauce 130
Egg spread 35
Filbert dressing 55
Garlic dip 23
Garlic quark 88
Gorgonzola and buttermilk
  dressing 55
Gorgonzola dip 130
Ham and caper sauce 102
Herb dip 23, 46, 102
Herby yogurt dip 34
Hot chile sauce 130
Kiwi sauce 140
Lemon mayonnaise 26
Mango sauce 137
Mascarpone cream 143
Mushroom sauce 123
Mustard and arugula dip 34
Nougat sauce 141
Olive cream 42
Olive sauce 69
Orange and cream dressing 55
Orange and cream sauce 123
Orange mayonnaise 34
Peanut dip 21
Pepper sauce 102
Raspberry sorbet 137
Rémoulade 27
Roquefort cream 42
Sun-dried tomato cream 42
Tartare sauce 27
Trout cream 27
Tuna pesto 68
Tuna sauce 26
Vanilla or cinnamon cream 137
Vanilla sauce 135
Vinaigrette 26
White bean cream 43

Wild garlic pesto 68, 88
Yogurt and lemon dip 23

Drinks

Coffee with Advocaat 149
Hot chocolate 148
Irish coffee 148
Irish cream 149
Latte macchiato 148
Mexican chocolate 149

Pizza toppings

Neapolitan style with anchovies 84
With arugula and Parma ham 85
With clams 84
With ewe's milk cheese and
  bell pepper 85
With four cheeses (quattro formaggi) 85
With salami and olives 84

Salads

Apple and bell pepper salad 65
Apple and cucumber salad 51
Arugula and pear salad 50
Chinese cabbage salad 51
Cucumber salad 101
Cucumber salad with dill
  and cream dressing 63
Fennel and orange salad 94
Frisée and carrot salad 65
Green bean salad 30
Green salad with raspberry dressing 71
Green salad with tomatoes 21
Iceberg and corn salad 45
Mixed salad 63, 129
Potato and bacon salad 94
Radish and apple salad 30
Radish and celery salad.......................................50
Raw celery salad 29
Red onion relish 45
Salad à la niçoise 50
Spinach and radicchio salad 51
Tomato and croutons 65
Tomato and cucumber salad 94
Tomato and scallion salad 30